EXECUTIVE COACHING

How to choose, use and maximize value for yourself and your team

Stuart McAdam

THOROGOOD

Thorogood Publishing Limited
10-12 Rivington Street
London EC2A 3DU

Telephone: 020 7749 4748
Fax: 020 7729 6110
Email: info@thorogood.ws
Web: www.thorogood.ws

A CIP catalogue record for this book is
available from the British Library.

PB: ISBN 1 85418 254 4

Cover and book designed by Driftdesign.

Printed in India by Replika Press.

Dedication

This book is dedicated to my mother,
Dorothy Courtice McAdam (1913-2004)

About the author

Stuart McAdam gained an MBA from Bradford University and a Certificate in Executive Coaching from Strathclyde University and The School of Coaching. He is a Fellow of the Royal Society of Arts and a Chartered Fellow of the Institute of Personnel and Development.

He has worked in both the public and private sectors, including lecturing at Nene College, Principal Officer with the local government employer's organisation and Head of Employee Relations at the Confederation of British Industry. More recently he spent eight years as a principal consultant with KPMG Peat Marwick, was Group Human Resources Director at M&G Reinsurance and Global Head of Human Resources, and Member of the Executive Board at Swiss Re Life & Health.

He is a Director of 365 Coaching and is currently working on 'The Insider's Guide to Outdoor Management Development'.

Acknowledgements

I am grateful to the many people who helped me assemble my thoughts on executive coaching – as they know this was at times a painful process for me!

They include Dilly Hallett, Mary Murphy, Wendy O'Shaughnessy, Mary Borba, Laura Dietrich, Anne Williams, Martin Powell, Jon Toogood, Chris Kane, Michael Rush, John Engestrom, Celia Baxter, Louise Redmond, Eva Ruzicka, Jim Barrett, Adrian Furnham, Liz Tate, Ruth Salazar, David Robertson, Richard Parker, Sara Burks, Peter auf dem Brinke, Sara Burks, Alex Swarbrick, Peter Jones and Tony Hipgrave. I would like to give Myles Downey a special mention for stimulating my mind on the potential power of executive coaching.

I thank those people and organizations that have allowed me to quote from their material: Tricia Bey at the School of Coaching, Gladeana McMahon at the Association for Coaching and Julie Hay of the European Mentoring and Coaching Council. The 'personal qualities' identified in the British Association for Counselling and Psychotherapy's Ethical Framework is reproduced by kind permission from Laurie Clark, BACP Chief Executive. The extract from the 4Square psychometric instrument is reproduced with permission from Jim Barrett and the British Psychological Society 'Code of Good Practice for Psychological Testing' is reproduced with their permission. I am grateful to Lee Salmon of the United States Department of Treasury, Federal Consulting.

Also thank you to Neill and Brenda Ross who made this book possible.

Contents

Introduction

Why this book?

'Join the world's fastest growing profession' reads the advertisement in the London Times. 'It's becoming **too** easy to set yourself up – almost like becoming a realtor in the states', says a very experienced coach. Although the skills of coaching have been practiced for centuries in one form or another, only more recently has coaching captured the imagination of a larger audience. As with many industries and professions experiencing rapid expansion, growing pains are inevitable. So are differences of opinion.

Moreover, type the word 'coach' into a search engine and what do you get? More than 58,000 listings for various types of coaches and coaching outfits. Additionally – and maybe not so surprisingly – a sponsored link for a bus company! Apt in a way since effective executive coaching is about getting the participant from A to B!

Despite this plethora of information, working out what a coach can do for you, or what you can offer as coach can be difficult. TV programmes showing almost instantaneous results from so-called Life Coaches don't help either. This is not to impugn the integrity of many life coaches, but to be realistic and recognize that TV programmes frequently go for impact rather than draw attention to the **process** by which coaching delivers results.

In the corporate world executive coaching is gradually showing the significant benefits it can deliver to a sometimes skeptical audience. And the recent upsurge of interest in the field of 'emotional intelligence' has increased the desire of many managers to find tools and processes to make it happen. Concerns over expectations not being met or confidences broken do exist, but there are very many great coaches delivering real and measurable benefit to their clients.

With these concerns and expectations in mind, this book aims to provide a pragmatic insight into executive coaching for those who:

- may be contemplating a career move and becoming executive coaches;
- are considering using the executive coaching process for their organization;
- are considering using – or asking their organization for – an executive coach; and
- those general readers who are interested in discovering what all the fuss is about!

Based on the number of recent – and recurring – press and other media pieces about coaching this is clearly a 'popular' area of interest. A cynic might suggest that coaching is not that popular – the idea of becoming a coach is! Certainly the concept of life coaching has captured the popular imagination. Some websites even carry the warning that 'life coaching is not a substitute for therapy or other medical needs'. Others compare it to having someone by your side as you embark on a brave new journey. In reality the processes used in many life coaching settings will be very similar to those encountered in executive coaching. The backdrop to the Executive Coaching described in this book is that it is being paid for by an organization to help an individual achieve their full potential at work.

Using my own criteria for judging the usefulness of management books this one will attempt to avoid homilies on the transformational experience this book will deliver. In my experience executive coaching CAN make a sustainable difference BUT you need both focus and desire to have this happen.

The structure of the book aims to guide the uninitiated, the knowing and the downright prejudiced through the key aspects of executive coaching:

- What is executive coaching?
- The organizational context
- Where executive coaching makes the difference
- How does it work?
- The coach as consultant
- What to look for in a coach
- What to look for as a potential coach
- Making this book work for you

Throughout the intent is to present topics and issues from the perspectives of coach, potential coach, purchaser and end user. It is predicated on the belief that all of us have potential and that coaching is a powerful and practical way of unleashing it.

In what is currently a completely unregulated area of professional advice, hopefully the book will prompt lots of conversation and maybe even conversion!

ONE
What is executive coaching?

This chapter picks up on the key facets of Executive Coaching. It explores the differences that exist between coaching, counseling and consulting, and examines the key components of the executive coaching process. Many are then dealt with in more detail in the subsequent chapters.

The need for coaching may seem self evident to an observer **before** the need is recognized by the person who would benefit; and the participant may well conclude "that was really much more useful than I expected" **after** the process has successfully concluded.

Notwithstanding the benefits of hindsight, based on numerous discussions with people in a wide range of organizations, there is rarely one start point to an interest in coaching. It may be triggered by an event or a crisis or a feeling that things 'could be better'. Indeed it may be seen as a route of last resort rather than an entirely appropriate means of seeking assistance.

In some ways, the term Executive Coaching is in itself something of a misnomer, and also the cause of some confusion. The book is not going to attempt to re-badge an entire industry but it may help you to think of what is being delivered as personal or team development consulting. It has also been described as fulfilling the role of 'executive confidant', which certainly captures the importance of having access to an impartial and non-directive source of help.

In simple terms Executive Coaching is:

The process by which the coach uses appropriate listening and questioning skills to work with the participant (coachee) to enable them to review and ultimately own solutions to issues upon which they seek resolution.

The issues being reviewed can range from coming to terms with a new role, to concerns over career direction, to dealing with feedback on performance and/or behavior which may at the time seem impossible to believe or to rectify.

It is the emphasis on helping the participant to learn for themselves that is one of the key differentiators from other approaches such as training or consulting. Fundamentally it is giving the participant the freedom and space to work on **their** issues and to identify for themselves possible approaches, solutions and measures of achievement.

Appropriately targeted coaching can deliver considerable benefits:

- Providing a sounding board for a new CEO
- Accelerating the rate at which an individual becomes productive in a new job or assignment
- Helping 'difficult' individuals achieve their full potential
- Significantly improving the ability of teams and individuals to deliver superior performance

However, there are also a number of barriers to getting this to happen. Misconceptions as to what coaching may or may not achieve, can get in the way. So too will the absence of a clear strategic perspective on the context of coaching. Equally it would be naïve to underestimate the views of potential purchasers:

- "It's touchy feely with no business benefit"
- "Clearly the coach had loads of empathy for the individual but zero understanding of our business needs"
- "Admittedly we have had problems retaining good people – but so does everyone else in our market"

Generally the coach is an outsider who can provide the means for a neutral approach. Although it has become more common for coaches to operate from within the organization, there are some important boundary management issues to resolve if this is to be successful. Indeed, boundary management is one of the defining issues in the delivery of effective coaching.

By working through the components of this working definition we are able to begin to build an overview of the way in which executive coaching fits together. This is of some importance, since the ability of the coach to maintain a 'joined up' sense of what is going on throughout the process is a key determinant of success. So whilst the participant may sometimes ask "Where are we going with this?" the coach remains connected to the overall purpose.

However, for the coach to remain 'connected' they will need:

- a model or approach that enables them to guide the coaching process; and
- the experience and competence to flex their approach in the light of their participant's needs.

In itself the intrinsic ambiguity of some elements of the process is one of the barriers to 'selling' coaching since many of us will be concerned to see – or at least know – what it is we are getting. The manager who likes to 'tick the box' may well see executive coaching as something you should just do and then move on and no doubt some inexperienced coaches can fall into the trap of pandering to this demand. To shift a potential client from this righteous completion syndrome requires effort. Without it:

- the process gets dumbed down to a pass/fail approach;
- the variety of skills required to successfully deliver effective coaching are underestimated; and
- the personal and organizational context in which coaching **must** be positioned are ignored.

As one CEO noted:

"I was particularly taken by the equation: performance equals potential minus interference, since it has always seemed to me that things get in the way of achievement ,but many of us are not really sure what they are or how to circumvent them. Or even if we do know, are we brave enough or have the appropriate skills to tackle them?"

It would be a major error to assume that such misunderstanding exists only in the eyes of the potential 'customer'. Many management consultants and professionals see coaching as a bolt-on to their advisory work. They may significantly underestimate the skills required to make coaching work, or see it as a complicating factor which may prejudice the likelihood of marketing and delivering their core offering.

So, what are the pieces of the coaching jigsaw?

Executive

To deliver 'what it says on the can' – or in this case, the title means the focus is on those individuals or teams with executive responsibility and account-ability. Generally the focus of Executive Coaches is on managers, directors or other high potential people. This does not mean that coaching cannot work for others inside an organization. Indeed, there is an increasing interest in developing coaching skills at other levels. There is, however, a risk that this can deflect from the development of senior managers who play a key role in shaping the culture of the organization as a whole. One Board concluded that whilst their subordinates might require several days training to begin to understand the process, they only required half a day!

Coaching

"Consultants tell you what to do whereas counselors just listen but they both demand fees for doing it" is a rather unkind and indeed stereotyp-ical view of the bookends of the coaching continuum. This is best described as push versus pull. The Push approach relies heavily on telling and selling whereas the Pull style creates an environment in which the partic-ipants learn for themselves, and identify possible solutions. In this context executive coaching clearly has more affinity with counseling rather than consulting.

Pull	Non Directive	Counselling
	Listening	
	Reflecting	
	Summarising	
	Asking Questions	
	Making Suggestions	**Coaching**
	Giving Feedback	
	Offering Guidance	
	Giving Advice	
	Instructing	
	Telling	
Push	**Directive**	**Consulting**

In reality, however, the coach needs a good grasp of each of the areas of intervention. An executive coach requires a portfolio of all these skills reinforced by experience, the flexibility to leverage these effectively and to be self aware enough to understand the boundaries within which they are competent to operate.

The fact that coaching exists and operates in this middle ground is no doubt a major reason for some of the difficulties coaching has encountered in establishing its credentials. When an organization engages a consultant there are generally a number of reasons for making the decision:

- The expertise does not exist in-house
- A transfer of know-how is expected from the consultant to the organization
- Internal resources are so stretched that outside reinforcements are required
- The consultant is seen as an external, credible source of advice
- The consultant has done it before – they have a track record
- The consultant sometimes has more weight with the board.

Generally there will be a specified need, process or project which requires consulting assistance.

Organizations rather than individuals generally commission consultancy. With counseling or psychotherapy the reverse is the case. In contrast to progress reports to a Board or Executive Team, the essence of counseling and psychotherapy is the opportunity for the individual to talk to someone in complete confidence. Although counseling may be short-term with a specific focus, it may have a more open focus and no defined end date. Psychotherapy is a process which may require a substantially longer commitment to work through a process which, by surfacing awareness of underlying patterns and how they present themselves in current relationships, can help the individual find their own answers.

Commissioning executive coaching may well be done by an organization, but it obviously requires the absolute commitment of the individual participant if it is to succeed. Does the organization or the 'client' know what they want – and what they are buying? As we see later, providing a coach for a 'maverick' will not in itself change their behavior to fit the corporate mould. And, as a potential participant are you clear about what coaching really involves? Chapter Two sets executive coaching into context alongside other personal development approaches and Chapter Three reviews opportunities for the process to make a difference.

The nearest compatible role is that of mentor which generally involves a WORK colleague rather than a neutral outsider in assisting the transfer of technical skills and providing an insight into other aspects of the organizations working practices. Another similar role is that of facilitator. Here it can be argued that coaching skills are actually being deployed – albeit for a short-term one-off event such as a meeting.

The coach

The coach is the individual guiding the coaching process. This may be on a one-to-one basis. Sometimes it may be for a team. Some larger coaching firms assign the role of lead coach who may conduct the entire coaching process him or herself. In other cases they may involve specialist coaches to work with the participant on specific needs or interests. This approach sees the lead coach as something akin to a general practitioner

A large number of executive coaching outfits have less than five coaches; indeed, many are one person firms. Here lies a potential dilemma since a determinant of success in coaching is **CHOICE**. Good practice will always allow the potential participant the choice – and right – to determine whether a particular coach is right for them.

There are in addition many Human Resource consultancies offering coaching services, in particular those which specialize in outplacement.

For a coach to truly deliver, a number of issues are non-negotiable:

- They need to know themselves, their strengths and limitations
- They need to have undergone a professional training programme with observation practice as part of the process
- They need to understand the organizational context in which coaching takes place
- They need to be passionate about learning both from their work and through subsequent review with an experienced supervisor.

The British Association for Counselling and Psychotherapy has identified the 'personal qualities' to which counselors and psychotherapists should aspire and these are included as Appendix One. They have real relevance for executive coaches and include "the ability to communicate understanding of another person's experience from that person's perspective" (empathy) and "the ability to assess accurately and acknowledge one's own strengths and weaknesses" (humility)1.

Some of the competencies required can de discerned from the feedback given about their coaching experience by these participants:

- ...helped me to make a difference for MYSELF by being the guy on the tiller... a touch or two in the right direction, but only when required.

- Enabled me to hold up the mirror and look into it, was very powerful. The apparent lack of direction was a little disconcerting at the start...I had anticipated someone telling me what to do.

- ...as a new CEO what was invaluable was the opportunity to have a completely neutral sparring partner with whom I could discuss anything.

- Helped my career by giving me the space to examine my real career needs and their impact on my family.

From the foregoing it will be obvious that excellence in executive coaching does not just happen. Without appropriate training and subsequent professional supervision, the management of the executive coaching process and the boundaries that surround it, cannot be adequately accomplished. These aspects are examined in Chapter Six, What to look for in an Executive Coach.

---

1   British Association for Counselling and Psychotherapy: ethical framework for good practice in counseling and psychotherapy

Questioning and listening

Many – if not all of us – are quick to provide an opinion on almost anything. What has been referred to as our 'always already listening' kicks in and without much thought or feeling an instant opinion is proffered. As managers or consultants we will have been paid to **decide** things. As experts or specialists our right to **direct** may have been taken as a given. Coaching isn't quite like that…

…Coaching requires the coach to look, listen and learn, and to do this by active listening and a more forensic approach to questioning than many of us generally deploy.

Reflection

By allowing the participant the freedom to step back and follow their feelings in a way that their normal working environment would never allow, new approaches to supposedly insurmountable problems begin to emerge. The literal benefit of reflection is exemplified by this comment! As a participant commented to her coach: "You're doing it again…holding up the mirror so that I do the work!" In a literal sense this is what coaching does; by creating a 'safe' environment the process empowers the participant to increasingly hold up the mirror themselves rather than relying on their coach.

Coaching is a process which takes time but gives you space

A process is more than a series of events; it is a coordinated programme with clearly defined objectives and anticipated activities. And whilst the gift of a few coaching sessions from a boss to a subordinate may superficially appear generous it ignores the importance of the time frame within which an individual can genuinely explore, learn and improve.

A 'typical' programme is likely to be based on a number of contact hours over a period of three, six or twelve months, or twelve two hour sessions over six months. It is important to recognize the power of the coaching process. Learning and adaptation takes place between sessions. It is simply not possible to compress this into, say two days full-time. Neither is it effective to have sessions separated by more than four or five weeks.

At times of economic pressure, coaching programmes along with other development initiatives frequently come under increased scrutiny. Sometimes a structured process is replaced by a 'pay as you go' approach. This is not without its dangers, since a sporadic, intermittent framework may well prevent the participant giving the process the focus necessary to achieve the progress they desire.

Face to face?

Some coaches offer telephone coaching and e-mail support as a matter of routine, whilst others avoid it completely or offer it as an 'emergency' service.

In any event, it is impossible to offer this form of back-up without the trust and confidence which has been built up over a series of face to face meetings. Thus, the approach of the coach who provided telephone support to a manager in West Africa was underpinned by a relationship developed through a coaching programme provided for the same individual in a previous role.

Many coaches claim not to enjoy telephone coaching: "encouraging reflection on a dodgy mobile connection is tricky" and "I find it difficult to pick up on what's **not** said." However, a number of organizations offering training for coaches observe that the virtual nature of today's business environment, coupled with the flexibility of e-mail and mobile telephony, is creating a market opportunity. This may well be true, but both the coach and participant will need to work on ensuring 'distance' coaching is appropriate for their circumstances.

Players and roles

The delivery of executive coaching within organizations has the potential to cause a remarkable amount of ill will if some basic issues around who does what for whom are not clarified at the outset. In no sense is coaching unique in facing this challenge. Since a significant proportion of executive coaches do not come from a corporate background a key issue is the extent to which they are able to 'read' the context and politics of organizational behavior. Anyone can describe themselves as an executive coach and the issues the potential purchaser needs to explore are reviewed in Chapter Six, What to look for in an executive coach.

In this book we are using the following terms:

- The **participant** or **client** is the individual or team receiving coaching.

- The **sponsor** is the individual who is corporately accountable for the coaching – and may be the line manager.

The role of the Human Resources function

The HR department is almost always at the center of the virtual hub which links the players and their roles. As such there is considerable scope for confusion if:

- there is no consistent approach to purchasing executive coaching across the organization;

- individual departments go their own way and make ad-hoc and sporadic decisions on people development issues; or

- some senior line managers see coaching as a 'personal' purchase with no need to seek approval for their decision.

Without some organizational consistency, opportunities to position coaching interventions may be lost and the key area of quality controlling potential providers may not adequately be carried out. In these days of e-procurement, rather than HR there may be an annual or triennial request from a central purchasing department to re-tender or pitch for work. However, it will nearly always be the HR function which coordinates the selection process.

From an external coaches' perspective the ideal HR function will be one which:

- proactively endorses the benefits of coaching;
- builds relationships with providers; and
- is prepared to offer opportunities to a range of providers rather than limiting themselves to just the one.

From an HR point of view the ideal coach will be someone who:

- provides regular updates without compromising confidentiality;
- is experienced enough to comment on other aspects of the organization from what they see as they go about their coaching; and
- does not attempt to sell-on additional work via their coaching client but uses agreed procedures.

The major point of friction seems to be centered upon reporting arrangements. "All we need to know is what's going on" observed one HR manager, adding "are any themes emerging which we need to know about?" This desire was countered implicitly by the coach who saw their role as "guiding my participant through what for them is proving to be an enlightening and at times an emotional experience. I don't want to compromise the outcome with anything other than a rather bland progress report at the moment."

Sensible reporting arrangements are possible which nip this potential conflict in the bud before it becomes an issue. A little reported but not infrequent variation on this theme is how work on the programme will be reported to the sponsor when a number of coaches are working with various clients in the same part of the business. "I give the basic information and no more" affirm a number of coaches. Since, in the UK market a substantial proportion of coaches are freelance, issues of coordination and agreed good practice arrangements for providing updates present greater challenges than in a coaching firm with full-time coaches.

In truth, words such as loyalty and professionalism are sometimes used in an exaggerated way by a small minority of coaches. Clearly one's professional duty of care is to the individual with whom you are working. However, a failure to recognize the expectations of the sponsor and their organization will do the participant a disservice in the long run.

There is an approach which bridges these potentially conflicting requirements that is simple and open. This is to agree in advance that at the completion of the process the coach will meet with the sponsor and review any organizational themes or issues which have presented themselves or been picked up by the coach's 'antennae', without in any way breeching the confidentiality of the assignment.

The role of the HR function as a provider of executive coaching is examined in Chapter Five.

Purpose

Sometimes the anxiety of all concerned to 'get on with the coaching' overwhelms the first and vital step in the coaching process: Why is the coaching deemed necessary and how will it be delivered?

The confusion may be compounded if there is uncertainty over the roles identified above and also who is to pay for the coaching. Sometimes the 'paymaster' assumes this gives them control of the process. Take the following situation:

A CEO contacts an ex-colleague who is now offering executive coaching.

"Jo, I'm worried about our newish Director of Quality. It's a new role we created about 18 months ago – it's really important to our survival – however the guy actually doing the job isn't delivering. He cost a fortune to hire from France but just isn't making the difference we expected. I've told him that a coach would really help his career development – and he seemed very pleased at the idea. He's expecting a call from you. I explained that we would pay for a few meetings between the two of you."

Spot any risks? From the perspective of the CEO and Director there are some substantial risks of differences in perception and expectation.

CEO	QUALITY DIRECTOR
"I need to solve a problem"	"I have been given a coach to accelerate my development"
"this is a quick fix or else"	"this represents a long-term commitment by my boss to me"

Rules of engagement

Without care this is where the 'Bermuda Triangle of executive coaching' takes the unwary to their doom! Whilst at any time two of the three parties in the coaching process may be talking, from time to time all three need to engage each other.

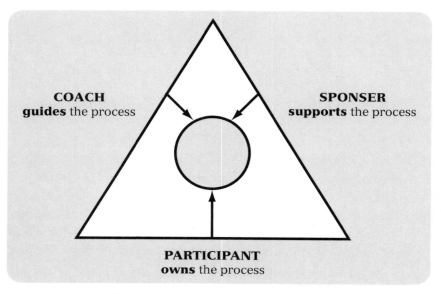

FIGURE 1: THE BERMUDA TRIANGLE OF EXECUTIVE COACHING

An important aspect to the coaching context is the extent to which a sponsor/manager is truly able to let go of the process. Experienced coaches know the importance of the sponsor to the process and will be assessing whether they have an ally, passive helper or the potential cause of some of the participants problems!

The figure below shows one way of anticipating the way the sponsor may behave. Many sponsors are more than happy to have a remarkably frank discussion about their own management style using this tool. Clearly its use needs to be prefaced with a 'health warning' that all this does is provide a framework for a discussion on what can derail a coaching programme and what it takes to make one a great success. Bear in mind that for the sponsor this may be their first contact with coaching. It may be viewed in the same way as nominating a colleague for a training course with little action on their part required before or after the event.

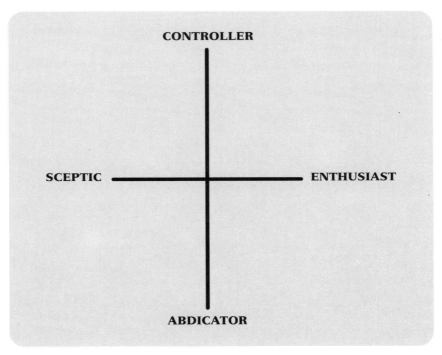

FIGURE 2: POTENTIAL REACTIONS FROM A SPONSOR

By reviewing with the sponsor whether they feel they are likely to 'abdicate' or 'control' and whether their view of coaching is that of a 'skeptic' or an 'enthusiast' it is possible to tease out how they see their role:

- In truth, would they prefer to tell the participant what they believe the solution to be?
- Are they prepared to let the participant own the coaching process – and indeed encourage them to do this?
- Do they understand the importance of making time available to continue working with the participant after the coaching process concludes?
- Are they fully committed to helping identify measurable indicators so that 'success' can be benchmarked?

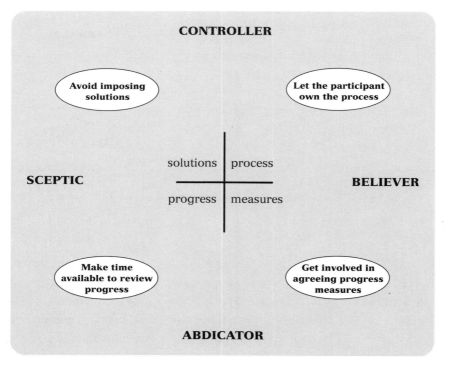

FIGURE 3: POSSIBLE OUTCOMES FROM A SPONSORS REACTION TO COACHING

Figure 3 pinpoints some **possible** outcomes in situations where sponsors have not been able to review the stages of the coaching process in advance. The trade-offs between process and progress, and measures and solutions are particularly important for the sponsor to grasp.

The conversation around these issues is an essential pre-requisite to a three-way conversation to do some risk mapping on barriers and risks to the process. The following often get raised; indeed they may have already been identified by the sponsor. If not, the coach needs to ensure that they are surfaced.

BARRIER OR RISK	RESPONSE
Insufficient time	Plan ahead; diarise schedule
Different perceptions of outcomes	Agree likely and desired outcomes at the start and report on any changes at agreed intervals
Disappointment with result	Ensure outcomes are measurable
Concern about the coach	Build opportunities for 'compatibility' reviews into the process

Something which is strictly neither a barrier nor a risk is the sponsor or client, or both seriously underestimating the impact of the process on the participant.

The process of helping people connect with their true potential may reveal a desire for a change in career. This may of course be within their current organization; for others it prompts a move elsewhere. In many, many more cases, however, coaching enables and empowers an individual to achieve their potential through their current role – with their employability significantly strengthened.

What will success look like?

The saying that "if you can't measure it, you can't manage it" clearly makes sense. Unfortunately, for some this equates wholly to numeric measures. It is of course also possible to measure soft areas such as shifts in behavior.

Organizational measures of success are often espoused in terms of key performance indicators or critical success measures. And the well-known SMART acronym guides the process of setting personal objectives:

- Specific
- Measurable
- Achievable
- Realistic
- Time bounded

However, is this sufficient in the context of executive coaching? The biggest risk is that a superficial goal will be created, although the framework described in this book actively involving the sponsor and the participant in initial goal setting helps alleviate this outcome. More significantly the 'discovery' session between coach and participant aims to surface what the participant **really** wants to achieve.

It is also important that measurability is not undermined at the expense of observability. A demonstrable change in the way a CEO manages meetings is more likely to be observed than measured. The subsequent improvement in decision-making may well lead to measurable improvement, but the initial impact of the coaching will have shown up in their behavior.

A useful approach is to ask the participant to map out their initial thinking on their goals and attempt to identify measures of success, using the template below. They may also be able to spot some of their key needs and help required from others at this stage, although this can be fleshed out and updated as the process proceeds. This template also reinforces the means of tracking progress being made by and between participant and coach.

LEADERSHIP GOALS	KEY NEEDS	WHAT'S REQUIRED FROM OTHERS/ ADDITIONAL SUPPORT	MEASURES OF SUCCESS
Create a high performance team	Be more self aware Gain the know-how to introduce performance related rewards	Introduce a performance management system that works!	Team targets exceeded
Improve team morale	Learn to let go/time management skills		Less missed deadlines! Clarity of expectations = less surprises!

As the process evolves – and self-awareness increases needs, requirements and measures will become clearer.

Creating a coaching environment

What the rather clinical dissection of the coaching map described above has done is enable a balanced view to be taken of the main components of the process. It can be seen that the interdependency of the components makes coaching a more complex process to deliver and **manage** than may have been assumed.

What this analysis understates, however, is the significance of the environment that an effective coach is able to create during the coaching sessions. Many participants have referred to this as:

- Having a safety net which gives you the freedom to think out of the box in an entirely supportive environment.

- Taking you out of the constant hassle of work and in a very real sense liberating you…. I didn't really appreciate this at the start since I was being encouraged to focus on what I really wanted… it was only as I became more comfortable with the sessions that I realized that I had the power to decide for myself.

It is the creation of an emotional environment within which the participant is at ease which builds the confidence to consider courses of action which may have hitherto been unimagined or rejected as being too risky.

TWO
The organizational context

This chapter reviews the ways in which organizations identify and respond to the needs of their people. The reactions of a sponsor to the suggestion that executive coaching may be an appropriate approach are examined as is the role of feedback in creating an awareness of need.

Identifying the need

It is worth exploring in more detail the ways in which coaching needs may surface in an organization. As we noted in the introduction, there is often no one cause. There are two levels at which coaching needs will initially be identified: organizational and individual.

On a macro level, how does the organization identify its people needs? This may happen in a number of ways:

- The business planning process explicitly asks for an assessment of the impact of people issues – such as skill shortages and anticipated labor turnover – on the ability of the organization to achieve its goals.

- Training needs analyses may be conducted on a regular basis to ensure a cost effective and consistent response to current and anticipated needs.

- Opinion surveys may identify issues relating to morale, labor turnover and the availability and impact of appropriate development programmes.

- The performance review process should be identifying areas of development for staff.

- Feedback from clients, directly or through market research; or the loss of an order, may heighten senior management concern at skill gaps.

In some quarters succession planning is seen as somewhat passé. Yet if an executive team does not have sufficient knowledge and information to complete the grid below in respect of their own direct reports, there may be turbulence ahead!

- Risk of departure

- Impact of loss

- Likely successors

- Stand-in

In part, the very act of a management team comparing perceptions of each others' subordinates is enlightening. All too often it may reveal:

- The absence of a common language to define performance and behavioral expectations.

- A wide variation in how superior or poor performance is actually assessed.

- Personal rather than objective assessments of performance and potential are allowed to go unchallenged.

- A willingness to suggest actions **others** need to take to improve the performance of 'their' people.

- Hearsay rather than observation used to identify strengths and development needs.

- No collective ownership of solutions.

A succession plan can provide a powerful impetus to review the strengths and development needs of the current senior managers. In the context of coaching the following are areas where a need may emerge:

- 'Difficult' individuals who are seen as having potential, but also seen as being unmanageable.
- High potential individuals where an external sparring partner would help them reflect on how to round their skills.
- People whom the organization is not sure it wants – or maybe isn't sure they really want to stay.

Feedback

On an individual level the performance review process is likely to be a major part of the needs identification process. Sometimes an individual will know a colleague or friend who benefited from coaching and open up the dialogue themselves.

But how do any of us know how well we are doing and how our performance and behavior is perceived? *"In this place you know you're doing well if you're not criticized"*, commented one senior manager in a multinational. Although increasingly sophisticated processes are introduced to support the annual performance review, getting and giving honest and open feedback to flow throughout an organization remains a challenge.

Some of the more common explanations of the barriers that emerge to thwart feedback are:

- A belief that giving a colleague feedback is unnecessary because 'they must know already'.
- Personal discomfort at having to 'hurt' colleague's feelings.
- Uncertainty as to how to give feedback in a constructive manner 'and anyway now's not the time'.

As a Partner in a consulting firm observed, *"I really should have given a colleague some feedback on a presentation. It wasn't as well structured as the client expected or required. However, the moment passed and the opportunity was lost."*

In reality most people are more grateful for feedback which comes with an opportunity to discuss and if necessary to redress the issues raised than to be left in ignorance. Ignorance is **not** bliss. However, all too often the processes which have been created to allow feedback are not up to the task, and the training and support necessary to make them genuinely effective are lacking.

Consequently, the extent to which they encourage a genuine dialogue on the issues underpinning an individual's capacity to develop is often questionable. Increasingly, some form of 360 degree feedback has been added in an attempt to allow more timely feedback. However, even these are generally an **annual** occurrence, viewed by many line managers as a chore.

The British Psychological Society[2] has noted that:

"In today's changing and volatile world organizations are continually looking for ways to improve performance and satisfy the demands of all stakeholders. Achieving this almost inevitably involves change, which then becomes the pivotal dynamic for success. For an organization to evolve the people working in it will have to adapt; and for this to be successful they first of all need to know what it is about the way they are currently performing that needs to change. This is where 360 feedback is playing a growing role in organizations through its ability to provide structured, in-depth information about current performance and what will be required of an individual in the future to enable detailed and relevant development plans to be formulated. Professionally managed, 360 degree feedback increases individual self-awareness, and as part of the strategic organizational process can promote:

- increased understanding of the behaviors required to improve both individual and organizational effectiveness;

---

2   British Psychological Society: 360 Degree Feedback Best Practice Guidelines

- more focused development activities, built around the skills and competencies required for successful organizational performance;
- increased involvement of people at all levels in the organization;
- increased individual ownership for self-development and learning; and
- increased familiarity with the implications of cultural or strategic change."

Some organizations have attempted to use 'new' technology to both support their drive for open feedback and reinforce their corporate values. Clearly the technology by itself can do little; and user training and support is the critical element.

The way organizations respond to these needs varies:

Highly centralized – in larger organizations economies of scale, a strongly embedded Headquarters culture or...may all produce a clearly focused – and centrally coordinated process for assessing and addressing needs. Quite often there will be a menu driven approach.

Global policy/local discretion – whilst there may be global processes for managing succession and organization wide management development programmes, other needs will be reviewed locally.

HR identifies partners/providers – any request for coaching assistance would be channeled through the HR team, or they will proactively suggest coaching as a possible approach.

Targeted at high potential individuals –bespoke development programmes may be created for high flyers.

Response to a particular problem – coaching may sometimes emerge as 'the last chance saloon' approach to an individual or teams perceived performance challenges.

Purchased by individuals – senior people may have their own personal development budget or, in the case of a CEO, will just do it!

Everything outsourced – with purchasing frameworks and providers determined by a third party.

Last but in no means least, is the **integrated** approach as illustrated below. The multinational company in question wanted to respond to the changes in career patterns, with flatter structures, the shift away from lifetime employment and significant acceleration in organizational change all having an impact. In career terms this was resulting in fewer promotional opportunities – with more time being spent in a particular post. In addition, the need for personal mobility was rising; and there was a need to increase awareness that in the future an individual might have a number of 'careers' with the same organization.

With this in mind, a review of current processes was undertaken and a new framework developed which aimed at optimizing both organizational needs and the preferences and capabilities of the individual. This included revisions to the performance review process, the introduction of more focused training and development programmes. Actually 'getting there' was seen as a combination of employee, manager and organizational responsibility. The employees were given responsibility for a variety of challenges including undertaking their own continuous development, and reviewing and revising life and career goals. To support this significant change, the intention was for managers to:

- encourage employees to take responsibility for their own careers;
- support realistic self assessment;
- provide clear and honest feedback on current job performance; and
- be open about organizational expectations.

For its part the company set about introducing tools and support for self-assessment and reinforcing the managers' role in career development. Clearly, a change such as this takes time, and even when progress has been made to create a corporate framework, the reaction of an individual sponsor as the **purchaser** of coaching remains pivotal.

How **do** they react? Initial interest and enthusiasm tempered by, "Great idea in theory, but what about…"

- logistics – "how much time will it take";
- funding – "there's no money left in my budget";
- awareness – "I saw a programme on TV about life coaching – terrible waste of money";
- history/track record –"we tried that once – it didn't work";
- priorities – "good idea, let's build it into next years plan" ; or
- joined-up HR (or the lack of it) – "surely one of those presentation skills courses will do the trick".

Before condemning these reactions as being too negative we all need to reflect on our own reactions to well intentioned personal development proposals. What does it take to persuade us? Moreover they may represent genuine concerns.

Logistics – creating the time to learn and reflect is an ambition of many senior managers who then add wryly, "although of course I don't have the time to get to that point!" Here lies a challenge for the executive coach in showing the significant opportunity cost of not investing time to explore whether things could, perhaps, be done differently. In many cases asking a potential sponsor or coach to describe what happens during a 'typical' working day is in itself enough to get their attention. *"Meetings, e-mails, conference calls, unexpected problems, media briefings, nothing seems to get done…"*

Funding – a robust cost-benefit case for introducing coaching is an important element.

Awareness – despite the increasing interest in coaching in all its forms, the focus upon emotional intelligence, and exposure to management consultants on a regular basis, most senior managers would be hard put to provide a clear description of how coaching works. This lack of awareness does not equate to resistance. However, there is no doubt that were executive coaching a requirement of getting the annual audit signed off, the take-up would be somewhat higher!

History/track record – has the sponsor seen coaching fail here or in a previous organization? Such concerns merit further investigation, since what was seen as coaching may have been something entirely different!

Priorities – In any organization priorities do shift. Indeed, flexibility may be imperative to survival. Potential initiatives do move up and down any CEOs wish list. Other organizations persuade themselves on an all too regular basis that this will be the year when every initiative is fulfilled; only to be disappointed as initiative overload brings progress to a halt. This can have a disproportionate effect on coaching with positive and negative results. The up side for coaching a project team in trouble may be seen as imperative; the down side is that the use of coaching may simply not be seen as important enough, so a decision is postponed. Certainly experienced coaches will know that there may well be a gap of months or years between an initial discussion and agreement to proceed.

As senior people move up and out of the organization, so may the sponsor be replaced, move on or become redundant. A new Director of Personnel may well wish to start with a clean slate and start a new selection process for coaches. They may also have been ignored in their previous role by a coach who deemed their influence of little importance!

The outgoing HR Director who told one of the providers of his redundancy, was greeted thus, "Oh that's terrible....who do I need to influence now?"

Joined-up HR – in too many organizations one fad follows another. Priorities around people management issues constantly shift and 'management by slogan' replaces common sense and value for money. In such an environment it would be surprising for executive coaching to be seen as anything other than the flavor of the month.

In organizations which do have joined-up HR policies and practices, the role of HR is likely to be focused on making line managers better managers of people. And coaching will not be seen as something to commend 'because the CEO likes it', but one of a number of potential interventions available, offering benefit to both the organization and the individual.

In addition, the current impetus given to the strategic role of HRM through human capital management represents an important potential shift in the focus of the function.

THREE
Where executive coaching makes the difference

This chapter explores situations in which executive coaching may be appropriate for individuals or teams, including some of the more common interventions:

- Assimilation coaching for newly promoted or appointed senior managers.

- Performance coaching for individuals and teams who may not be achieving anticipated results.

- Career coaching for people deemed to have the potential; to progress to the highest levels in the organization.

- Providing line managers with coaching skills to enhance their capability.

Below a range of situations is outlined. This is by no means an exhaustive list. In reviewing these opportunities whether as a potential coach, sponsor or client, readers will no doubt have their own sense of what will or will not work for them.

Assimilation coaching

Many CEOs agree that their first few months in their new role were somewhat challenging! They also acknowledge that challenge is the thing that motivates them. That asked, "Where does the person at the top look for guidance?":

- The Chairman?
- The Board?
- The HR Director?

To varying degrees all of these individuals can provide part of the solution. However, the first 100 days in a new role is often seen as a make or break phase and many organizations now see the coach as intrinsic to the success of the process. Interestingly few search firms seem to have made a success of linking their recruitment expertise to the coaching needs of the newly installed (ex) candidate.

The presence of a sparring partner with whom to discuss how things are going – or anything else for that matter – has clearly made a difference for many senior executives. Unfortunately their own belief in the process does not necessarily mean that they will be persuasive advocates. One CEO noted, *"I knew my CFO needed a coach. I offered to stump up the fees but he said the timing was wrong"*, and that was that.

Given the significant outlay that generally occurs in searching the external market for new talent or even benchmarking internal contenders against the outside world, the cost of failure is high all round. No one disputes the pressures of a new high profile role. So, why the hesitancy to invest a relatively small amount more to mitigate some of the risk?

Explanations abound:

- Having found the 'ideal' person, some form of post-recruitment euphoria sets in and assumptions are made about the ease with which this individual will do what's required. As most of us have come to realize, unless and until you've actually got the job there is no way of being absolutely sure what surprises and challenges await.

- "If they want feedback they're experienced enough to ask for it" - Chairman's perception of a new CEO and other Board colleagues.

A number of CEOs have commented that the provision of a coach was something they negotiated as part of their package. In other words, they sought it rather than were offered it. Indeed, some have paid for the coach themselves.

> "What I thought I needed was the classic sparring partner to test out my ideas on strategy. I had some grandiose plans for shifting the direction of the business. As things turned out, I was unprepared for the difference between my management style and that of my new CEO. I was able to work through my likely – and indeed actual – reactions to challenge and pressure. I hadn't realized how averse I can be to what in my eyes is 'conflict'. My coach helped me adopt a proactive approach to managing my boss which involved working through his likely reactions and developing strategies to handle them. Although I had done a number of psychometric tests at various points in my career, this was the first time I really had the opportunity to think – and feel – what they really meant to me."

Divisional CEO

Performance coaching

Whilst assimilation coaching may have no specific purpose at the outset, performance coaching will be focused on identified and agreed needs. However, the role of the coach may initially be to conduct some preliminary work with the sponsor and client to help them share their thinking on what's really going on.

An individual was bluntly told by their line manager that their team management approach was seen as akin to bullying by some of their subordinates.

The message was that unless s/he did something about this they were unlikely to be promoted, despite their considerable technical skills and their undoubted talent.

The individual was offered a coach via their HR department and made a preliminary choice on the basis of CVs supplied by a coaching company currently working for their organization. The first meeting focused on how the participant felt about their situation. Words such as hurt, upset and shocked featured, along with a deep concern not to be seen as an unreasonable person. Initially there was a view that *"if I'm not promoted, so what?"*

Subsequent sessions used a variety of techniques to help the participant focus on what was actually going on in their relationships with others. What was being said, in what manner and context, and how their behavior may have impacted on the team and other colleagues.

What proved to be the most useful technique was the use of a journal to record as much or as little of anything that happened and mattered in between coaching sessions. This proved extremely helpful in enabling an action-replay of the events with the opportunity to retrospectively focus on what had occurred and to discuss the appropriateness of the behavior.

What also made a considerable difference to the participant was the impact on colleagues when they implanted changes discussed at their coaching session. *"At the last...meeting I made a conscious effort not to go in with all guns blazing. I was still able to make my point – which surprised me – and I felt better for it."*

Career coaching

Organizations continue to invest huge amounts in increasingly sophisticated competence models which frequently earn the software supplier significantly more than the ROI on the project. High potential people still get derailed – or derail themselves. It may well be that the sophistication of the tools overwhelms discussion of the actual process. Organizations need effective succession planning processes if they are to acquire the talent required for survival and success.

Executive coaching can provide a means for such individuals to test out career choices in terms of impact and implications:

> *A 30 something labeled as 'high potential' by their organization, and with a significant ambition to become a CEO within ten years, was contemplating an internal transfer from their financial marketing role into an investment banking role. They saw this as a way of enhancing their experience and internal marketability within the parent organization. After a wide range of 'what if' conversations with a coach they made the move. Keeping in touch with the coach on an intermittent basis over the next six months it started to become clear that the role was not all that had been expected. Whilst there was a significant intellectual challenge, the culture and style of the operation did not match the individuals own preferences and personal style. With their coach they worked on what this meant in terms of future moves and the participant was able to develop a plan for an internal job search. This proved successful with a move made to another division within six months, whilst maintaining good working and personal relationships in the investment business.*

An interesting insight into an individual's perception of what career coaching may be expected to achieve is shown in the case of someone who, having purchased coaching off-the-shelf to help them change career, became aggressive during the first session. They did not want *"to waste time reviewing my past – all I want is advice on what to do next and the salaries that go with some jobs I'm considering"*.

'Difficult' people

"He's a bit of an animal at the moment – no tact if you know what I mean – but we believe he has a future here" was a comment made to one coach about a prospective client. The good news is that there was at least some recognition that without some action the individual was at risk – in many cases the person concerned is left to their own devices.

The potential coach and participant met and the coach reviewed the participant's perception of their current role and their impact on colleagues. What emerged was a picture of an individual who was very much caught up in the technical nature and challenge of their role. They didn't see their behavior as unreasonable; rather as a means to an end. When asked whether they had ever contemplated using a different approach, which would still get the job done and maybe gain more support from colleagues, they expressed interest, noting that, "I've never really been given any guidance on this sort of thing – I've just got on with it". Subsequent coaching sessions focused on helping the participant review the range of choices available to them in dealing with others. The process also included the use of a number of psychometric instruments and it was also agreed that the participant would attend an open management workshop on team management.

This combination of discussion, practice, feedback from the questionnaires and reflection caused the participant to devote considerable time to what they really wanted from their career. Acknowledging the insight they had gained, they recognized that they might well have been perceived as difficult to manage and a 'know it all' in the eyes of their peer group. Notwithstanding this, they did have the ambition to progress as a manager and worked with their coach on a plan to help this happen. The first stage was to get involved in a project team, to be able to gain more experience of working as part of a team.

'Here to stay?'

This category presents a number of ethical issues. Whilst we might all agree that giving someone help in working out what they really want is a laudable idea, would we be prepared to commission such help as their manager? Maybe not. Certainly a proportion of individuals who buy themselves some Executive or Life coaching may well wish to explore what comes next in their life and work without their employer being involved.

In a corporate context what is unacceptable is to offer coaching to an individual about whom the organization has concerns in the vague hope that it may encourage them to go elsewhere. This inevitably has repercussions, since once word gets around it can at a stroke destroy any confidence in the coaching process.

What needs to happen is an honest conversation about the way the organization views the individual and his/her prospects. An offer of coaching to help them identify options for the future can be an appropriate way forward.

"I was grateful for the opportunity to conduct a career review with an outside coach. There were things I was able to discuss that hadn't been possible with my own boss. I was also encouraged by the fact that the coach did not come from the firm the company used for outplacement!"

This individual did, in fact, choose to leave their current employer.

Coaching during projects

Within organizations a huge amount of activity is now focused on projects. Successful implementation can make or break careers. Millions are invested in setup, start up, monitoring and tracking. Yet despite this, overruns produce huge opportunity costs and the price of getting things back on track can be substantial not only in cost terms, but in the disruption caused to other activities. Projects also have a nasty habit of creating turf wars between functions and can produce remarkably dysfunctional behavior.

This is, to say the least, strange, since there are some **certainties** about projects. They all have the following in common:

- A defined start
- A defined end
- Deliverables which are clearly understood
- Allocated resources

Despite this, Project Management – or rather the process by which projects are managed – often fails to meet expectations. In both the literature on this key area and as described by experienced project managers the most common challenges and barriers to a successful outcome are:

- Unclear or unrealistic expectations
- Unrealistic technical complexity
- Top down direction with little room for bottom up contribution
- Anticipated resources unavailable or inappropriate for the task
- Poor coordination producing constantly shifting priorities
- Inadequate communication processes and skills
- Role confusion between sponsor and project manager
- Failure to separate the distinct phase of the process: initiation, planning, execution and control, and closure

In some cases this is further complicated by the absence of an organization wide protocol and consistent adherence to it. Whilst project management training may be mandatory for line managers, it somehow seems that Board members and other senior people somehow just don't have the time to attend.

The Avanza Partnership[3] has identified the separation of project management and benefits delivery as crucial. Their approach identifies and manages the interdependencies between the project, the delivery of benefits and business as usual.

Project leadership:

- Responsible for project delivery
- Involved through the duration of the project
- Proposes rollout approach and delivery timeframe
- Identifies and manages risks and issues that impact project milestones

---

3   Avanza Partnership presentation

Benefits steering group:

- Accountable for benefit delivery, e.g. adopting new ways of working
- Involved throughout the project and after project closure until benefits are delivered
- Agrees rollout approach, commits to benefits and timeframe for delivery
- Identifies and manages business risks and issues that impact the delivery of benefits

They argue that managing projects is not the same as managing benefits. Although the delivery of business benefit is the driving reason for initiating a project in the first place, often a project team and the business lose sight of the benefits case as the project progresses.

Many of us will have experienced the sentiments expressed by one CEO when a major project started to consume significantly more resources in both capital and people terms than expected, "you don't stop rowing when you're in the middle of the ocean".

Indeed, stopping a project may be infinitely more difficult than gaining agreement to begin.

Which is where coaching comes in. First, how might a coach get involved? Areas could include:

- Acting as a sounding board to a benefits steering group or project leadership team
- Providing coaching support for the project manager
- Acting as a sounding board for the project sponsor
- Providing a sparring partner for the project team before progress reviews with the board

The benefits would include the opportunity to review, in an objective way, progress and challenges with an individual with no other connection with the project. This in itself presents an interesting challenge. As a Partner in change consultancy noted, "the idea sounds fine – but the impartiality required makes it unlikely that we would sell the idea. On the other hand, if a client told us they wanted to use a coach to assist the process we would be unlikely to reject it...indeed, how could we?" It should be acknowledged that a number of large change management consultancies do go to some lengths to train change team members as facilitators in an attempt to overcome some of these challenges.

> "Looking back on it, what we had was a battleground of competing aspirations on the part of the Group and the operating Divisions on the one hand, and functional rivalry between our IT team and the consultants. Would a coach have helped...it's difficult to know for sure but more openness about what we didn't know would have made a tremendous difference at the start. The project sponsor would also have benefited, since they clearly thought their role was to give a regular pep talk rather than understand the ramifications of our plan."

Manager of an aborted project

Inbound coaching

In some ways this presents a similar challenge to assimilation coaching. It encompasses assistance given to inbound international assignees and those who have joined a company by virtue of merger or acquisition. Surprisingly perhaps, these groups of individual are often assumed to be resilient – or expensive enough – to be able to look after themselves. However, failure to integrate them speedily will have significant cost and organizational implications.

The international assignee

Congratulations! You have just made the move of your life – new job, new location and same company. Yet is it really the SAME company? Things just don't work the way they used to back home – decision-making is unimaginably slow and the personal chemistry between colleagues seems very cold.

The challenge for the new incumbent is who to talk to about these concerns. Although s/he will be given tax and relocation advice, very rarely is there recognition of how long it may take to settle. The assumption very often is that 'expensive' assistance with logistics and housing will make it possible for the new job to look after itself.

Someone in a new role may be hesitant to talk to their new boss in case this raises concerns about their commitment to the job; they may also suffer self-doubt about their concerns – after all they and their family were given a useful induction programme to the new country back home. Their partner has enough challenges at the moment sorting out a possible interim role for the duration of the assignment and their previous manager isn't likely to be interested.

In these circumstances, a coach can significantly help a newcomer by providing a regular opportunity during the first few months to act as a sounding board for these concerns.

> "I was offered a move to another region which was both flattering and daunting. I felt I was making a significant contribution to the operation in X, in part because of the time I had spent establishing my credibility. However, the move to Y was probably a one-off opportunity. If I didn't take it I would never know whether I was up to the challenge. My husband and I had about a month to decide and we both concluded the move would be great for the children, but more of a challenge for us. We were right about that...luckily the HR department offered me a coach. Initially I saw this as a means of tapping into someone from outside the company to discuss things that on one level might appear a bit trivial; however what emerged were my deep seated concerns about my future."

International Assignee

Coaching during mergers and acquisitions

Those readers who have been on the receiving end of the consequences of M&A activity may not have found their integration into 'Newco' that easy. On a rational level things may appear very positive; a bigger role and enhanced package maybe. However, they may simply not feel comfortable with the new set-up. This can be particularly acute where an organization has done its best to avoid a takeover. Despite survey after survey reporting that people issues are one of **THE** significant determinants of the success or failure of M&A, opportunities to mitigate them sometimes pass unnoticed. This failure frequently begins at the due diligence stage where eagerness and anxiety to move may thwart recognition of:

- the impact of the deal on the culture of the acquirer and the acquired;
- the distraction of internal power struggles upon client relationship management;
- the absence of a common language to describe success and failure; and that
- despite a vast pool of energy, people require time to work out their sense of place in the new environment.

Once again it may be more appropriate for a 'neutral' to provide a safe environment to explore these feelings and help the individual focus on their future and the reality of their current position.

A recent Conference Board®[4] survey 'Managing Culture in Mergers and Acquisitions' found that:

"Top management needs help. Nearly half of respondents strongly agreed that CEOs and other senior leaders could use advice and counsel in understanding cultural and personality issues in M&A. These are top executives

---

4   The Conference Board: Managing Culture in Mergers and Acquisitions, Lawrence Schein, 2001

with M&A experience observing the behavior of other top executives having problems of personal pride, territoriality, narrow fiscal focus, and inattention to cultural alignment and organizational morale. Such matters are not easily raised in board meetings and in executive or management committee meetings. Politically it can be enormously sensitive, if not dangerous."

"Initially I was highly skeptical of the benefit (of having a coach), but after a few sessions it suddenly struck me how bitter I must have appeared. Once that registered I started to see the significant benefits (the takeover) presented to my career. My coach helped me to give myself permission to celebrate our past achievements and get closure… then get on with my new role."

CFO of acquired company

A convergence of M&A activity and project management presents itself in the shape of the ubiquitous integration teams used to deliver the accretive value so beloved of deal-makers. As a visible manifestation of the 'new' business and its values, the teams can be a great showcase. Sometimes they are disrupted by internal argument. No doubt some of this is created by simple communications breakdowns, which in turn recreate the perception one side has of the other: *"typical of that lot – they're so arrogant; you'd think they had just taken us over!"*

In some ways the hesitation to see coaching as a value-added activity is understandable. There may be an extremely detailed plan and process for ensuring all aspects of the integration are delivered according to plan. Yet it would be a rare plan indeed that accurately predicted every possible eventuality. What distinguishes success from failure is the ability of a team to take a deep collective breath, review their position and determine what now needs to be done.

"I'm not sure we had a coach in the classic sense, but we benefited on one particular occasion by involving an outside party who was a former colleague from another organization in which our team leader had worked. At this point in the integration process we didn't seem to be getting enough

buy-in from each other. The 'coach' helped us achieve much more openness by taking us through a series of iterative discussion frameworks which enabled us to surface our feelings about the situation in a constructive way. Two things surprised me the level of anger and frustration that had hitherto been internalized by all of us; and the relief at realizing we all still had a shared belief in our end goal, but had somehow lost our way."

Integration team member

Coaching to non-executive directors

One Human Resources Director dismissed the notion of coaching for non-executives on the grounds "if they need that, we don't need them". However, in 2003 the UK Financial Reporting Council published 'The Combined Code on Corporate Governance'. This Code has significant implications across the whole field of Corporate Governance, requiring that:

- "...all directors should receive induction on joining the Board and should regularly update and refresh their skills and knowledge." In this regard, "The chairman should ensure that the directors continually update their skills and the knowledge and familiarity with the company required to fulfill their role both on the Board and on Board Committees. The company should provide the necessary resources for developing and updating its director' knowledge and capabilities."

- "The board should undertake a formal and rigorous annual evaluation of its own performance and that of its committees and individual directors."

The Code has significant implications for the entire field of corporate governance. Given the requirements now laid upon Chairmen and Board Members, three questions arise:

- Is there a role for the executive coach as an adviser to the chairman and/ or individual board members?

- Is there a role for the executive coach in transferring coaching skills so that the chairman and board members can better meet their responsibilities?

- Are there sufficient numbers of executive coaches with the right mix of skills and experience to take on this challenge?

Coaching during outplacement

During the 1990s successive waves of upsizing, rightsizing, downsizing and restructuring have created organizational needs which the outplacement industry has not been slow to exploit. A wide range of firms now provide a spectrum of offerings which range from advice and support on every aspect of redundancy. This extends from individual, and sometimes open-ended, support for a senior person made redundant, to short group programmes on C.V. writing and interviewing skills for more junior staff.

The skills required of the outplacement counselor are generically very similar to those of the executive coach, and senior managers are very often provided with a coach to act as their guide through the process, with other colleagues delivering specialist input on needs or issues identified. There is a need to raise a health warning here, albeit a minor one. Given that the employer is paying for this service and that the individual about to use the service is in a vulnerable state of mind, the opportunity for the individual to be allowed to 'shop around' for outplacement assistance is not that common. Clearly an employer able to buy outplacement assistance at 'bulk' rates is likely to be unwilling to accede to such a request.

This does not mean the chosen outplacement provider is unable to provide a choice of coach once the individual joins the programme. Indeed, the need for many outplacement organizations to have a flexible cadre of executive coaches able to respond to short-term needs is a significant source of employment for coaches.

Coaching teams

Top teams can sometimes exhibit the characteristics of a dysfunctional family to an extent that would shock their subordinates. Behaviors which would not be tolerated in a departmental meeting are sometimes excused on the grounds that "xx is a character, but technically superb...". In part the explanation may lie in the fact that someone does not get onto an executive team by being a shrinking violet. By there very nature these are competitive people, who may not always see the need to give others 'airtime'.

This can be a particular problem as Executive Teams become increasingly international in composition. There may be significant challenges for a team which operates in one language when the mother tongue of the majority of team members is not that language.

The absence of agreed and demonstrated standards of behavior may be due to:

- No benchmarks against which to measure performance.
- Concern on the part of some team members that 'raising soft issues is a good way to get yourself sidelined'.
- Team members may have no alternative approach to offer, and consequently remain silent.

The triggers leading to more introspection on the part of an executive team on their own behavior and performance may be:

- The arrival of a new CEO with experience of a more collegiate approach.

- Problems such as project overruns, governance issues and inade-quate due diligence on acquisitions forcing a review of how decisions are made.

There are no doubt many, less traumatic circumstances in which the need for outside help may be considered, as these examples illustrate:

- A Board was increased in size and the CEO was concerned to ensure the existing and new members acknowledged each others challenge in operating together.

- A functional Head became aware of significant problems within her team. They included resistance to new ways of working and a high level of criticism of colleagues 'behind their backs' rather than to each other.

- The manager responsible for an HR team, which had coordinated a large-scale redundancy exercise and was subsequently restruc-tured itself, wanted to rebuild morale and provide a means of allowing his team to acknowledge the past.

- An internal audit team was concerned to move away from an 'accounting' focus to an approach which combined the team audit expertise with the evolving requirements of a corporate governance environment. There was both excitement and fear about the opportunities this shift would create.

In these and other situations the approach the executive coach will need to employ will vary, and the tools and processes available are explored in the next chapter.

Enhancing manager's skills

The examples illustrated above are not uncommon, and neither are situations in which an understanding of the process and delivery of executive coaching can enhance the understanding and capability of individual line managers:

- to give and receive constructive feedback on their performance;
- in becoming more alert to ways in which a subordinate could do with help, and having the skills to lend assistance;
- heightening the manager's interpersonal skills;
- making the manager more aware of opportunities in which a coaching approach could help resolve a conflict; and
- more generally adding to the repertoire of competencies available for managing oneself.

In macro terms, the prevalence of large-scale change makes the case for the deployment of executive coaching skills difficult to refute. Paradoxically it may be the label 'coaching skills' that has prevented some organizations exploiting the benefits of providing such training. Re-branding such development as 'performance improvement skills and strategies' may bear bigger dividends!

...And the ones that get away

For those potential coaches who are identifying many opportunities for their coaching skills, a health warning is in order at this point. Despite the plethora of real situations in which the executive coach can demonstrably make a difference, the market is still in its relative infancy and buyer resistance can be strong.

Given the wide variety of approaches organizations take in determining their people needs, it will be clear that a coach seeking to gain entry to any organization will find diligence and resilience important! They need to be diligent in being thorough in their research into the organization, and resilient in accepting that it may take time and a number of rebuffs to gain an opportunity to present their approach.

The key question to be able to answer is: who really makes the decision to purchase?

However, a recent Conference Board®[5] report identified derailers, which if not addressed would pose an obstacle to an executive's future success. They included:

- Risk aversion
- Personal arrogance and insensitivity
- An overly controlling leadership style
- Reluctance to deal with difficult people issues

One of the paradoxes of the executive coaching market is that individuals with these very traits may be your target. Convincing them of the need to change is, and will remain, a challenge!

---

5   Developing Business Leaders for 2010, The Conference Board, 2002. Research Report, page 6

FOUR
How does it work?

This chapter looks at the cycle of an Executive Coaching programme and the tools and processes available to the coach:

- Preparation
    - Agreeing on the need
    - "How will we work together?"
    - "What will success look like?"
- Delivery
    - Coaching teams
    - Tools and techniques
- Closure and sign off

Preparation

Agreeing on the need

As we saw in the previous chapter, there are two parts to this. Initially there will have been some form of request from an organization or individual expressing interest in learning more about coaching. A meeting or meetings will have taken place to ensure coaching is an appropriate response to the stated needs, and a proposal written and delivered. In some cases this will be accepted as-is. In other situations further discussion may be required.

Despite a formal agreement to proceed, the coach now needs to meet with the individual participant. This meeting allows an informal opportunity to talk through how coaching works and address any concerns the participant may have. The most frequent topics to arise at this stage are:

- How do you report to my manager?
- What should I tell my colleagues?
- How long have you been doing this?
- What does it really involve?
- What happens if I change my mind?
- Is this really necessary?
- Where and when will we meet?
- What if I fail?
- I've not really got any questions – can we just get started?

How do you report to my manager?

Not unreasonably, someone whose manager has suggested coaching is going to have some concerns about confidentiality and reporting back. The reality is that the coach and participant need to agree on a process for feeding back outcomes – ideally driven by the participant. There may also be arrangements to feed back basic information such as sessions completed to the HR function; if so this should be made clear. It is important to recognize that what is commonplace for the coach may be disconcerting for the participant.

It is also sensible to clarify that anything discussed with or produced for the participant, is not disclosed without their agreement and that test results for example are theirs.

What should I tell my colleagues?

Generally the answer will be to be as open as you wish. However, there may be circumstances where a participant will be more cautious. Someone experiencing difficulties with their team management skills may feel embarrassment, fear or uncertainty and this may underpin their question. Generally the advice is to have people tell colleagues they will be meeting an external consultant for some scoping meetings as part of a possible project. Although not wholly true, this removes the burden of explanation from the participant's shoulders until they are comfortable with the process and see that they are getting something from it. There is invariably a point in the coaching process at which the time is right for them to be open with colleagues. Obviously it is important that the individuals' manager is aware of and agrees to, this approach.

How long have you been doing this?

This question or variations on a similar theme, are asked for many reasons. It is a way of checking out the coach's experience, track record and credentials. In other words, for the participant to be comfortable that the coach **has** done this before and that it worked!

What does this *really* involve?

This may be a return to the theme of confidentiality or an attempt to compare the process to other events in the participant's career. This may include:

- Having been given inadequate feedback on tests

- Fearing the coaching process is an assessment center in disguise

- In many cases simply doubting that what has been described may make a difference!

What if I change my mind?

One aim of this first informal conversation is to emphasize to the participant that what happens next is entirely up to them. They are able to withdraw from the process at any point. Once the process is started and the sessions get underway this is unlikely, although occasionally a participant may request a change of coach. It can be difficult for the participant to feel able to raise concerns, since they may perceive the coach to be the 'expert'. The use of paper-based feedback can help overcome this reticence and this aspect is explored more fully below.

Where and when will we meet?

However large the office, conducting a coaching session in a participant's home territory isn't a great idea. Boardrooms or other meeting rooms are a much better alternative, so long as they are free of interruptions and other distractions such as screens showing the latest market prices. Most participants are more than happy to use another room, but they do need to be alerted to this requirement in advance!

Larger coaching firms are able to offer the use of their own premises, which can help some participants distance themselves from the everyday challenges of their role.

Is this really necessary?

From the coach's point of view this is a great question, since it enables a conversation around what coaching can do to help someone really focus on those things that are 'getting in the way'.

What if I fail?

An individual may be at a particularly low ebb when considering – or being confronted by the need for – coaching. They may be having difficulty coming to terms with feedback on their performance or their apparent insensitivity to others. It is imperative therefore, that they are made aware that executive coaching is giving them the opportunity to take stock and then move forward. Rather than pass/fail it represents an opportunity for a win in terms of increased awareness and commitment to take action.

I've not really got any questions, can we just get started?

Having an eager participant is good news – as long as they are aware that coaching is not a quick fix. More challenging is the participant who has not yet fully committed to the process and 'just wants to get this over with'.

The outcome of this session will be agreement from both coach and participant that they believe they will be able to work with each other. However, a key piece of this contracting process is a reminder to the participant that they own the process and if they have concerns they should raise them.

How will we work together?

Once there is agreement to begin, a first and usually longer, formal session takes place. In the words of one coach it's for us both to review the question, "What do we need to know to be able to work together?" Others refer to it as the 'discovery' session.

Underpinning the whole coaching process and this phase in particular is the creation of an environment in which the participant is able to learn for themselves. But what is learning and how does it take place?

A useful framework for guiding this conversation is the FADO model – this bears no relationship to the Portuguese song style of the same name. However, one web site defines Fado as 'being born of unique sentiment, of a soul that can't be explained but only felt', so maybe there is a link after all in recognizing that learning takes place on a level just beyond current understanding.

Improve **focus**	Increase **awareness**
Harness **desire**	Spot **opportunity**

The following questions can help get an open dialogue going:

- Where would improved *focus* help you?
- What *opportunities* do you feel are open to you?

- What might heightened *awareness* mean for you?
- What do you really *desire*?

These have relevance to participants, irrespective of the type of executive coaching they are receiving. A newly appointed CEO and a high potential staff member will both have ideas and feelings on the opportunities that confront them. Of course the individual's perception around the attractiveness of the opportunities is another issue. Moreover, the concerns that initially present themselves may not be the real barriers to the participant's fulfillment of their true potential.

What the FADO model enables is a non-directive look at where the participant is now and where they feel they may – or may not – be going. It can be likened to the first stage in the process of unfreezing, often employed in change management. Here the initial emphasis is on acknowledgement of feelings. It also sets the scene for personal learning, which coaching will enable in part through the process employed and by the tools and techniques deployed. It also enables the participant to not only describe what 'success' **may** be, but to go a stage further and actually visualize what it will look and feel like.

One senior manager responded thus to FADO:

> *"I'm in a new role which excites me very much because of the opportunities it creates to build our franchise in new locations. That's the opportunity. The desire is to succeed and for the business to succeed. As for focus and awareness… that's the bit I sense is my biggest challenge. How am I going to both fulfill the role of a Board level job, handover to my new number two – who was previously my equal -and keep tabs on how the business is performing?"*

Used in a team context, the model may surface potential areas of tension very quickly. The following were raised by members of a team:

- "I think we need to focus on developing an integration plan as quickly as possible and then get on with it… we have been given a mandate from Board level, which gives us a lot of clout."

- "I've got a somewhat different need at the moment. If I'm honest I'm pleased to have been chosen for this team but recognize that I need to understand my – and our – role better. We're not here just to represent the business we work in, are we?"

What will it take for the team to learn? The basics of effective learning require the process to:

- be active – a consequence of doing something rather than passively waiting for guidance;
- allow clarity to be gained from both information and experience;
- be one which builds on existing understanding;
- take place at a level just beyond current understanding; and
- recognize that learning cannot occur without reflection.

A variety of approaches are adopted by coaches to help learning happen. One very effective approach is based on the **GROW** model. As the name implies this model supports coaching conversations focused on:

What do you want?	**G**OALS
What is happening now?	**R**EALITY
What could you do?	**O**PTIONS
What will you do?	**W**ILL

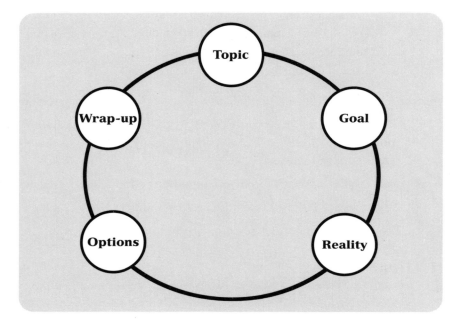

FIGURE 4: THE GROW MODEL

The use of the GROW model in action is explored below.

What will success look like?

This aspect links with the questions posed by the GROW model. As we have seen, executive coaching is taking place for a purpose:

- For a senior manager the purpose may be to help them achieve their potential as a senior executive.

- For a high potential individual it may be focused on providing an opportunity to acquire additional insight into their own behavior.

- For a new CEO it may include the provision of a non-threatening and non-challenging environment within which the participant can think through alternative courses of action.

- For the leader of an integration team it may be providing a sounding board for the participant to use to test out different courses of action and set realistic goals.

- For an international assignee it may be to provide a process by which the participant is able to acquire information and feedback on how their management style is perceived by others.

It is the non-directive nature of the executive coaching process that enables a participant to identify and own the solutions to these goals for themselves. As the example below illustrates, a key facet of effective executive coaching is a non- directive approach as opposed to the provision of advice.

Delivery

A group of coaches, practicing what they preach and reflecting upon the approaches they make use of to 'make it happen', identified the following components as vital:

- Ensure the participant retains responsibility.

- Remember that the participant does the work and the thinking.

- Follow the participant's interest.

- Use questions for understanding not interest.

- Listen.

- There should be minimum interference from the coach.

- Keep the end goal in mind and check back as necessary.

- Don't allow the focus to narrow down too quickly.

- Have a clearly agreed goal.

The Association for Coaching[6] has published a competence framework of Core Coaching Capabilities which expands on these essentials.

---

6   Association for Coaching: Core Coaching Capabilities

Knowledge: As a coach you need to know:

- What coaching means and what distinguishes coaching as distinct from other learning and helping roles
- What the coaching process involves and what coaching models underpin your role as a coach
- Where coaching fits within the wider developmental processes (particularly within organizations)
- What personal and professional capabilities the coachee needs to develop
- How to manage the coaching relationship and to set clear boundaries
- How people respond to, manage and resist change
- How people learn and adapt coaching to suit different learning styles the limits and boundaries of ones own practice

Skills: as a coach you need to be able to:

- Actively listen and communicate at different levels
- Employ your intuition
- Creatively ask questions
- Influence with integrity
- Give feedback artfully
- Be empathetic in the face of setbacks
- Demonstrate confidence in self and coachee
- Be compassionate
- Work openly and collaboratively
- Challenge the coachee
- Help coachee engage in problem-solving

- Facilitate goal setting and generation of own strategies
- Focus on action
- Inspire persistence
- Act in the best interests of the coachee
- Network and access resources
- Manage self
- Demonstrate passion
- Act ethically and with the highest integrity

Behaviors: as a coach you should:

- Demonstrate empathy and build rapport
- Promote and facilitate excellence
- Inspire curiosity to open up new horizons
- Encourage self-discovery
- Act as a role model
- Be non-judgmental
- Possess a sense of humor and use appropriately
- Value diversity and difference
- Show tact and diplomacy
- Maintain trust and confidentiality
- Signpost client to other sources of support
- Seek opportunities to build client's confidence and self esteem
- Critically evaluate own practice
- Engage in continuous professional development
- Share learning with clients and peers and the wider coaching community

It takes quite an effort to do that many things in a 90 minute conversation! In practice there are a number of frameworks which coaches are able to deploy to coordinate these processes. The GROW model is a good example. However, by itself it is just a framework – a mechanism to guide the flow of conversation and reflection. So what needs to be added?

The School of Coaching[7] identifies a number of areas critical to the coaching process:

- Helping others understand themselves and the situation more fully so they make better decisions.

- Creating an environment where others aren't afraid to have a go and become fully involved in the activity.

- Believing in the untapped potential within individuals and encouraging the development of the whole person.

- Understanding the organizational pressures at play in the workplace and taking them into account to get things done.

Within these four areas a range of techniques need to be deployed to 'make it happen'. The example below shows some of these:

BEE is the newly promoted managing director of an operating division. He has worked for all his working life and gained promotions to successively bigger roles over the last twenty years or so. This move puts him in charge of a business which he knows very well. His new manager Norm is an American who has been in the post for a year or so.

A range of business issues have come to light very recently. Bee and his boss have a telephone conference most days and it is clear that Norm does not like surprises.

---

7   School of Coaching: Coaching Development Indicator

Bee is referred to as P (Participant) and his Coach as C below:

C   *What issue would you like to review today?*

P   *I'm not sure; there's a lot going on...I've got a problem with the accuracy of our monthly reporting. The most recent report only landed on my desk an hour before it was due to be sent to the group. We've also just started the business planning cycle, which I've contributed to, but not actually led before...so there's a lot going on around me.*

C   *Tell me more about what you mean by going on around you.*

P   *I guess I mean around rather than wholly guided by me.*

C   *Thanks.*

P   *Where was I? Oh yeah, lots going on without me necessarily controlling it. Apart from that I need to be on the ball since the telephone conferences with the boss are a bit of a challenge. I think it's because we're not meeting face to face. I'm not sure I always read him properly and I suppose I'm feeling vulnerable because I'm new to this role.*

C   *Tell me a bit more about that.*

P   *Well I've been in this role a few months now and I'm still learning, clearly. I'm still being surprised and that makes me edgy...so does the reaction of Norm.*

C   *Anything else?*

P   *You probably noticed that I've said nothing about my team – other than indirect criticism over the late production of a report – and nothing about our clients. That worries me, since in the past I've been described as someone who genuinely walks the talk and has been obsessive about client management.*

C   *May I summarize the points you've made?*

P   *Feel free.*

C   *There appears to be a number of concerns for you at present:*
   - *the telephone conferences with Norm*
   - *late reporting*

- insufficient people and client focus

- your new role… or rather what you feel you need to do to be in control.

Have I got that right? Is there something I may have missed?

P   *I don't think I have a concern over having my new role – actually I'm very pleased to have got the job – it's more about doing the job to the best of my ability.*

C   *Thanks for that. Which is the one that you feel it would be helpful to work on here today. It may help to give each one a score indicating your perception of the need to review it now. Zero is low, ten is high.*

P   *O.K. I reckon late reporting is a six, but I have some ideas on how to deal with that: getting my focus back is a three; my new role is not a problem, rather a concern; but if I don't get a grip of the telephone meetings I will have a problem soon!*

C   *So shall we focus on the telephone conferences?*

P   *Sure. Shall I tell you a bit more about them?*

C   *Yes.*

P   *In fact it's not the teleconferences as such – I use them all the time. It's more about Norm's behavior during the conference.*

C   *Tell me some more about that.*

P   *Well, it sometimes feels as if he's out to get me. I'm sure he isn't but that's how it feels.*

C   *What makes you so sure?*

P   *Other than during these meetings he's very supportive.*

C   *If you were him how would you view these meetings?*

P   *Probably not as meetings, I would see this as a transaction rather than a relationship driven event. Ideally review what's up, and then move on. I'd also like proposed solutions to any issues identified.*

C   *Is that how you currently see your contribution?*

The coaching session then moved through the other phases of the GROW model. It emerged that Bees approach to these meetings could be tightened up with a more transactional focus; and it was agreed that he would try this approach next time and report back on the consequences.

The next meeting was viewed by Bee as an improvement on the previous ones: "It seems to me that from Norm's point of view these meetings are no big deal – I may have been building them up into something they were not.

What's happening?

In the short example above, the initial temptation of those with a superficial sense of what coaching is, but no training or supervised practice in the delivery, is almost certainly to:

- proffer advice as soon as a solution emerges in the mind of the coach based on their beliefs, rather than letting the participant work it through; and

- fail to listen for meaning and become judgmental rather than allowing the participant to generate options for action and test these out for themselves.

The good practice approach is to use a non-directive approach to:

- clarify understanding;

- use summaries to help the participant;

- use open questions to draw out the participant's feelings; and

- allow the participant to assign priority to the issues for discussion.

The grid below is a useful aide-memoir for this approach.

Rapport	Probing
<ul><li>openness</li><li>responsiveness</li><li>active listening</li></ul>	<ul><li>suspend judgment</li><li>clarify</li><li>identify specific issues</li></ul>
Insights	**Taking action**
<ul><li>ensure understanding</li><li>reflect and clarify</li><li>establish themes</li></ul>	<ul><li>gain commitment</li><li>ensure ownership</li></ul>

However, it bears repetition once again, that these skills need to be acquired and honed in a safe training environment before they are deployed upon a participant.

Coaching teams

To put team coaching in context it is helpful to make some distinctions:

- **Team building** is the process used to get people to work together effectively and jointly aligned to a purpose. This is generally an event, ranging from a few hours to a few days duration.

- **Team facilitation** is the process used to enable discussion to take place within a team, and will usually be used for one or a series of team meetings.

- **Team coaching** is the process by which a team is enabled to achieve results and is a process oriented intervention with a longer timeframe.

In a team setting the coaching practices described above take on a somewhat different focus. Clearly with more than one person involved the role of the coach shifts from ensuring the participant owns the process to balancing contribution, so that one participant does **not** dominate the process. It is also important for the team to understand that, collectively, they own the process. It is not unknown for a team, deliberately or not, to attempt to put the responsibility for the outcome on their coach rather than themselves.

Sometimes a coach will be invited to work with a team as a consequence of an existing coaching assignment. A CEO with whom the coach is working may see a broader involvement with the executive team as beneficial. In these circumstances the game rules around confidentiality and feedback are obviously very important. Before any work is contemplated it is important to get the buy-in of the team to the process and purpose. This is often accomplished through a briefing workshop on what coaching is, how it works, and the benefit it can deliver. This creates a first – albeit not the only – opportunity for any concerns to be raised. It is also important for the team to agree on the reason for the exercise and to have a common expectation of what success will be for the team.

As mentioned earlier, the challenge may be to ensure the team is clear about the process of coaching, since they may be expecting someone to come along and facilitate their meetings, "so that we become more effective". Here the coach, or more accurately the facilitator, is seen as the person who will make the difference rather than the members of the team having to do anything other than listen!

An assignment which led to a substantial shift in team behavior, had as its purpose:

"Increasing our effectiveness as a team by reviewing how well we communicate and work with each other and thereby enhancing our effectiveness as an organization."

It was agreed that the coach would build up a picture of current practice by interviewing the team members individually. A report would then be prepared for discussion by the team and their coach. To encourage open discussion, the report would not attribute comments to individuals.

A structured approach was utilized, which included issues such as:

- What was seen as good or bad about current communications.
- The extent to which each member felt they knew sufficient about each others jobs and responsibilities.
- Whether there was common agreement around the critical success factors used for reporting.
- Individual confidence in the business planning process.
- Feelings about the level of openness in team meetings.

What emerged was a wide range of concerns about the style of team meetings, rather than the substance. There were also concerns that the style of meetings – described by one participant as "fragmented with people switching on and off, rather than remaining engaged throughout" – impacted on decision-making. It also became clear that, although a number of respondents saw these concerns as important they had not felt able to raise them in a meeting. One individual saw the reason for this as his mother tongue not being English; others argued that as long as the items on the agenda were covered there was no need to "rock the boat".

The coach presented the findings to the team and invited reactions to the findings. On this occasion the team as a whole had agreed to be the sponsor, so the CEO had no prior briefing before the meeting. During this meeting the coach used a variety of techniques which are common in team coaching:

- Since this was the first time the coach had seen the team together, observing interactions between the participants and the dynamics of their behavior was particularly interesting. Although they had all responded in the pre-meeting interviews with descriptions of how they perceived the teams' behavior, the coach was now able to observe any gaps between perception and reality. As with any team meeting, varying forms of influencing behavior were on display, with varying levels of success!

- As with coaching an individual participant, listening remains a key skill; in a team situation the challenge is to ensure that the coach builds up an understanding of the whole group, not just the most vociferous members.

- More active skills in the form of 'gate keeping', to balance contribution and drawing connections between the comments made team members', were also used.

The key challenge for the coach is to remember that they are just that: the coach. So in this initial meeting it was very important not to direct the team towards a particular conclusion or set of actions. In the event, a wide range of opinions were expressed, with some individuals more vociferous than others. The intent of this review meeting was to provide an opportunity for the team to start the process of reflecting on the findings. For one participant this was a challenge, since they assumed that during this meeting it would be possible to either agree or disagree with the findings and move on.

It was agreed that two hours would be set aside at the start of the next executive meeting in a month's time to decide what, if anything, the team was going to do. The coach, with the CEOs permission, asked team members to get in touch in the interim if there were any aspects they wanted to discuss.

A number did this, with one expressing interest in getting some coaching for themselves. The coach and CEO also reviewed the findings and the reaction to them. Both acknowledged that a majority of the team were veterans of many 'team events' where much was promised, but little delivered. There was also a realization that the way team meeting were currently conducted were transaction rather than relationship focused. Any move towards a relationship driven approach would take time and, in part, would require the team members to see that a more consensual approach would actually deliver benefit to themselves and the organization.

Closure and sign off

Interim reporting

Let us for a moment assume we have an ideal sponsor who supports the coaching process; who appreciates the need for confidentiality but also recognizes that they have a role to play in working with their colleagues on the agenda that emerges from the executive coaching process. What will they legitimately expect to learn from the process as it unfolds?

They will certainly expect 'regular updates and will no doubt have a perfectly natural curiosity about what is going on! Herein lays a challenge. For without clarity on what a regular update is, and a timetable around the reporting, curiosity may lead to impatience.

Closure and sign off

Towards the end of the coaching programme it is important for the coach to help the participant work towards closure. Closure embraces a number of activities:

- Reviewing whether the goals of the process have been met.
    - It would be surprising that, if any of the goals had not been met, this were to become apparent at such a late stage.

Without an agreed tracking process this is a possibility. More realistically, it needs to be acknowledged at the very start of the coaching process that it is essentially a work in progress, and supports, not supplants the development plan for the individual.

- Identifying what the participant will be doing as a consequence.
  - For example, a meeting for the participant, coach and sponsor to go through the outcomes; or for a CEO to outline their personal learning to their executive team.
  - It is also important for coach and participant to spend time reviewing and, if appropriate, updating the participant's medium to long term development plan.
- Considering the highs and lows of the coaching process.
- Ensuring that any corporate arrangements for sign-off are appropriately completed. This is clearly important from an organizational perspective and is looked at in more detail in Chapter Eight. If there are not any arrangements, it is very much in the interests of the coach, sponsor and participant to create them!

It can be argued that closure begins as soon as the process commences, with the emphasis clearly on the participants' ownership of the process. What needs to be avoided at all costs is the emergence of a dependency relationship.

Tools and techniques

We have seen the wide range of skills a coach should be able to deploy to help their participant begin to understand themselves. But is this enough? Self awareness is a great thing, but on occasion we will all need some evidence to support what we sense to be true. Consequently, it would be unusual for a coaching programme not to include the opportunity for the participant to learn more from the use of psychometric instruments and observed behavior. Essentially, this element of the coaching process provides input on not how you seem but how you are. It creates a snapshot of personality, values and abilities which help the coach formulate questions upon which to test hypotheses.

Many coaching programmes use psychometric instruments as an intrinsic part of the process. Some coaching organizations will only use coaches who are qualified occupational psychologists who consequently are able to deploy a wide range of approaches. Others sub-contract this part of the process to an occupational psychologist; whilst other coaches will be qualified to use a specific range of instruments.

Unfortunately, the short-hand for psychometric instruments tends to be 'tests' which conjures up the notion of pass or fail. The word test probably also reminds participants of the many hours they or their children may have spent revising for exams. They may also make a connection between skill and aptitude tests taken as part of the assessment process for a job.

In practical terms, however, there are three areas of importance:

- the context in which a coach uses them;
- the range of approaches available; and
- how the feedback gained is utilized and connects to the coaching process as a whole.

Some coaches offer their participants the opportunity to complete a battery of tests very early in their programme. The rationale is generally argued as being to benchmark the participant and to provide pointers for the programme as a whole. This can be very useful indeed, since some instruments will provide the coach with a significantly improved sense of what makes the participant 'tick' and they will be able to flex their coaching style and approach accordingly. In other cases the coach will offer the opportunity later in the programme.

Whatever the timing, the participant needs to understand the purpose of the instrument and be comfortable about this. Very occasionally there are rumors of a sheep dip approach to test batteries with little apparent connection between the instruments used and the needs of the participant. More common is the charge that the coach restricts the range of tests used simply because these are the only tests they are qualified to administer! Unfortunately, most participants are unlikely to have enough technical knowledge to challenge this; the British Psychological Society's guidelines on the use of tests provide a useful reminder on this and are included in Appendix 2.

Range

The range is wide and ever growing! There are many well researched tests of intellectual, personality and interest factors. One of the best-known is the Myers Briggs Type Inventory – better known as the MBTI® which not only gives the participant a window on their own behavior and the drivers of it, but can also offer the coach valuable pointers about the responsiveness of the participant to different coaching approaches.

An interesting psychometric is the '4Square Management style' inventory®. which uses **two** versions of the same questionnaire to produce a mirror of both the participant's own responses and those provided by a colleague, usually their manager.

"The purpose of the 4square exercise is to become more aware of yourself by comparing your perceptions of yourself with those others have of you. Perceptions and behavior can alter with self-awareness and awareness of others."

As with any other instrument used in coaching, the key purpose should be to elicit discussion, reflection and learning:

"The most important learning is likely to arise through discussion with respondent(s) of the differences between the questionnaires. Do not seek to justify or blame. Most benefit is obtained when you or your respondent, seeks to understand how and why differences in perception arise:

1. Discuss different results in charts 1 and 2.

2. Compare differences on individual statements from the questionnaires.

3. *Discuss any other differences in perception.*

4. *How are your previous perceptions of yourself different from what you expected?*

5. *Why might your respondents perceptions differ from your own?*

6. *Have you become aware of how to deal with any misunderstandings?*

Observed behavior

Just as psychometrics can open up a window for the participant, so can feedback. Feedback may be the stimulus for an individual to recognize that they have a challenge, or indeed an opportunity, and that it is time they did something about it. In other cases the absence of open and constructive feedback may have been a barrier to seeing the need for change.

Yet, just as there is a need to explain the nature of psychometric instruments, so is there a need to be very clear about the role of feedback in the coaching process. Whatever the purpose of the coaching, at the initial stages there may be understandable reticence on the part of the participant to asking colleagues for feedback on their performance and behavior. Indeed, their colleagues may not even be aware that they are receiving coaching. Neither may the early stages of the coaching programme have created sufficient trust or confidence on the part of the participant to see it as adding value.

A middle manager asked for coaching as a consequence of feedback from their team on the *"inflexibility of their management style"*. Upon meeting the sponsor and potential client, the coach suggested that it would be valuable for him to use a structured approach to gather feedback from a range of colleagues and others, such as internal clients. Both the sponsor and participant had some initial reservations about this. The sponsor believed 'our culture should be open enough for us not to need this'; whilst the participant became concerned that there was some hidden agenda behind it.

The participants' concerns were assuaged by a reassurance that the findings would be absolutely confidential between himself and the coach; with the coach also pointing out the potential value of the opportunity to get this insight. Both accepted the coach's observation that sometimes it is far easier to be open through an intermediary – in no sense how we might like things to be, but nonetheless how they are. Notwithstanding these concerns, there was agreement that one of the aims of the coaching was for the coach to work with the participant to help them review with their team their feelings about the feedback and what, if anything, they proposed to do as a consequence.

The approach used by the coach was a series of forty-five minute interviews with eight people nominated by and agreed with, the sponsor. Those taking part were guaranteed the anonymity of their responses, but were aware that the results would be fed back to the participant in detail. The key questions underpinning the interviews were:

- Describe X's strengths as a manager
- Describe X's development needs as a manager
- If you had the power to get X to change just one aspect of their management style what would it be?
- What would you like more of from X?
- What would you like less of from X?
- If you had one gift which would modify X's behavior what would it be?
- If at this moment you had the opportunity to send X a message what would it be?

What emerged from these interviews were some clusters of concerns underpinned by the desire of most respondents for X to succeed. The concerns focused on poor delegation, perceived inconsistencies in behavior and a desire for X to loosen up a bit.

The reaction of the participant was initial concern that the comments had not been made to him directly and the coach helped them explore why this might be the case. The participant started to realize their behavior may have been a contributory factor and that the absence of effective progress meetings with their manager was giving them no real opportunity to reflect on how they were 'showing up' to the team. They also recognized the supportive nature of much of the feedback.

This led to a meeting with their manager at which the participant was able – as the owner of the findings – to ask for more support in the form of time! A subsequent meeting with the team resulted in the team developing a protocol of behavior for everyone based on rights and responsibilities.

Neuro Linguistic Programming

NLP is an approach which emerged in the 1970s which is used by a number of coaches. It helps participants explore how we all make sense of our experience and how we interact with others.[8]

Keeping a journal

Writing reports, taking minutes at meetings and responding to ever-increasing volumes of e-mails may dissuade many managers from seeing writing as a development tool! Yet for some participants the real breakthrough in their self awareness will emerge as a consequence of reviewing their journal with their coach.

The journal enables a retrospective review of what the participant did the consequences and their subsequent reaction. It enables them to reflect on what they notice about what occurred from a distance.

---

8   For a comprehensive review of NLP see "The NLP Coach"

Role reversal

Getting the participant to role play the person they perceive as an adversary or barrier to gaining agreement to their plans can significantly heighten awareness of their own behavior. This can work in situations such as:

- A CEO having difficulty establishing an effective working relationship with their Chairman.
- A CEO finding it hard to manage a direct report.
- A project team preparing to give an important presentation to the main Board.

Putting oneself in the position of the other person can help the participant create some distance from their immediate feelings and allow them to learn more about how a particular behavior, or pattern of behaviors, 'lands' on the other person.

Non-directive?

It's worth noting that non-directive does not equate to non-involvement. There will be occasions during the process when, with permission, the coach will proffer their thoughts on the way in which a particular approach contemplated by the participant may 'land'. Indeed, this use of business savvy may well be the reason the coach was selected.

There is an important paradox at work here. It relates to the 'buzz' a coach gets from a participant emerging from the process with **their** solutions to **their** challenges. However, no matter how great the adrenalin burst when this happens, the coach still needs to remember that they are there to provide the means for the participant to acquire insight, not to provide direction!

FIVE
The coach as consultant

From the foregoing chapters it can be seen that coaching needs to have a context – both individual and organizational. Whilst the range of skills deployed by the coach emphasize aspects of both counseling and consulting the process is identifiable in its own right. If we think of executive coaching as personal development consulting, it helps to position the process as something more akin to traditional consulting in terms of many things including relationship management, managing expectations and clarity around deliverables and scope.

These are not always things coaches have necessarily been trained to manage, nor may they have had experience in managing these things from a consultant's side of the fence. They may also not be seen by the participant as desperately important – after all they expect their coach to COACH them not provide updates and reports. However, the management of these aspects can make or break a coaching relationship and it is upon these that this chapter focuses.

Initial contact

As discussed in previous chapters, when interest is expressed in a coaching assignment the coach needs to determine what's required. The coach needs to identify whether the request represents a genuine need for coaching, who the likely sponsor is, and the number and type of participants.

We have seen that the importance of clarity around the **why** of a coaching need cannot be understated. Whilst there may be compelling reasons to go ahead, it may be that there are reasons why the coach cannot personally proceed. Conflicts of interests created by ongoing work with an existing participant(s) in the same organization or a competitor, could be issues here.

Returning for a moment to the distinction between sponsor and participant, it is important to separate the competing expectations at work. The participant, as the recipient of the coaching will ultimately get the personal benefit. Sometimes the impact of the coaching process and the quality of the coach creates a situation in which the participant forgets the original terms of reference. Whilst this may well be a compliment, any requests which go beyond the original agreed terms of reference such as additional coaching sessions, need to be approved by the sponsor. Coaches who carry on regardless, despite having agreed a time budget with the sponsor, are likely to walk into difficulties sooner rather than later.

And what of the sponsor? As the person or institution commissioning and paying for the work they clearly have an interest. The checklist below will help a coach – and indeed an individual who may need their sponsor's approval to proceed, to avoid some of the potential pitfalls:

QUESTION	SPONSOR	PARTICIPANT
Who initiated the enquiry?		
Does the sponsor have authority to proceed?		
What are the sponsor's needs?		
What are the participant's needs?		
What is the relationship between participant and sponsor?		
Has the participant any views on what success will look like?		
Where does coaching fit with other initiatives?		

QUESTION	SPONSOR	PARTICIPANT
Do both have a realistic sense of the work involved?		
Do either have any prior experience of coaching?		
Who is the competition and why have you been asked to propose?		

In many consulting projects making time and resources available is a significant challenge. Paradoxically the fact that money is being spent on coaching certainly engages the sponsor's interest. However, this does not always equate with a realistic sense of what may be required from them in terms of commitment and interest. The participant needs both focus and desire if they are to both make time available for coaching and, more importantly, for the reflection and learning which occurs between sessions.

Once upon a time there may have been a remarkably informal approach to engaging a coach. However, these days your sponsor will almost certainly conduct some form of beauty parade and certainly expect a written proposal with detailed terms of reference.

The beauty parade

Here we look at what needs to happen from the coaches' side of the fence. Whether a sole practitioner or a representative of a larger firm, you need to know:

Complexity of situation	Problems Opportunities
Client objectives	Stated Perceived Deliverables
Tasks	Description Methodologies Deliverables Milestones
Resources	People Time/access

In other words, what's needed, by when, at what cost and delivered by whom? Sometimes the coach may have been sent, or responded to, an invitation to tender. This will have provided some of the information identified above and, maybe, an indication of the context within which coaching may be required. However detailed the information provided, there is no substitute for a face to face discussion on what's really needed.

Terms of reference

The proposal outlines the coach's understanding of the sponsor's requirements:

- Background to the coaching programme
- Summary of sponsor expectations

- What will be delivered and how this will be achieved

- Statement on confidentiality of information

- Time and resources required

- How success will be measured

- How progress will be reported

- Fees and cancellation arrangements

Here's an example:

Coaching agreement

Xxx Consulting and Coaching Ltd (hereinafter referred to as the consultants) and (organization name) hereinafter referred to as the sponsor who are party to this agreement, agree that the coaching period of xxx hereinafter referred to as the client is to consist of two sessions per month over a minimum period of six calendar months commencing...

The coach is ...and face to face sessions will be held at a location to be agreed between the coach and client. The first session is to be of three hours duration and subsequent sessions will be two hours. The coach will provide timely telephone and e-mail support if requested by....The sponsor is to use their best endeavors to ensure that time is made available for the client to attend the coaching sessions.

In addition it is proposed that (coach) and (client) meet with you at agreed points during the coaching programme to discuss progress and issues of relevance to the process.

Continued over...

The purpose of the coaching is...

All parties agree that the content of the coaching sessions remains confidential to the coach and... The coach undertakes to terminate coaching support to... should s/he decide during the term of this agreement to leave the sponsors employment.

- In consideration of the above the sponsor shall pay the consultants £x per month for a minimum period of six calendar months, plus expenses.

- Telephone support will be charged at £...and e-mail support will be charged at £...

- This agreement may be terminated at one calendar months notice or by mutual agreement.

Many, but not all coaching assignments include the use of feedback tools and psychometric tools so the costs of these needs to be clearly included along with an estimate of the time required to interview other colleagues if some form of peer feedback is required. In addition, the proposal above explicitly recognizes the need for time with the sponsor.

It is not the intent of this author to justify, or indeed be in the vanguard of an attempt to increase fees! Notwithstanding that, this is probably the right point for a brief word about fees. The range is significant, going above £3,000 a day in some cases. However, remember that coaches need to prepare and subsequently reflect upon each and every coaching session. So a 2 hour session almost certainly involves one or two additional hours.

Value for money

We have explored the situations in which coaching can deliver results. However, at some point in the commissioning process there will be a discussion on value and cost. The coach needs to be in a position to identify:

- The cost of taking action.

- The risk of doing nothing.

- The benefits to be gained and the certainty that action will lead to gain.

- The timeframe within which the cost-benefit will be measured.

A benefits matrix is a useful tool for the coach to deploy:

	Financial	Non-financial
Quantified	An improvement where financial impact is clearly identified and measurable	An improvement which has a non-financial but measurable impact
Non-quantified	An improvement which has a financial impact that cannot be accurately estimated	An improvement which represents noticeable and real progress but in a way that cannot be measured accurately

A coach working with the Board of a professional services firm produced the following assessment.

	Financial	Non-financial
Quantified	**Financial** Improved financial management with Board taking active role in management of billing across the Firm	**Non-financial** Improved identification of cross-selling opportunities
Non-quantified	Potential revenues from development of cross-discipline products	Improvement of firm-wide IT processes will enhance productivity

The coach also needs to be able to show how executive coaching, rather than another initiative will deliver these benefits. The cost-benefit matrix below shows an example of this:

Cost-benefit

First order benefits	Second order benefits
First order benefits • Develops the individual • Strengthens talent pool • Delivers short-term performance improvement	**Second order benefits** • Strengthens skill base • Creates a more resilient management team
First order costs • Coaching fees	**Second order cost** • Opportunity cost of undertaking coaching

What can go wrong?

The coach has a client with a supportive sponsor and agreement to proceed as indicated in the proposal letter. So what can possibly go wrong? Hopefully nothing, if the following points are borne in mind.

Delivering on time on budget

Executives are invariably busy people. A coaching session may not always be their number one priority. So the coach needs absolute clarity as to how failure to show will be treated or charged.

The coach on the other hand is unlikely to impress their client if THEY are late or frequently change arrangements. Some coaching is agreed on a piece-meal rather than a programmed basis and this can both impede the power of the process and cause logistical problems.

What clients don't like is surprises. Items unexpectedly appearing in an invoice, or an invoice appearing months after the conclusion of the coaching invariably leaves a bad impression.

Scope creep

It is flattering to be asked to do more work. Indeed, much executive coaching is sold by word of mouth. The motto for the coach is "confirm everything in writing".

A related issue for the coach is not so much scope creep as handling repeated requests for updates by the Sponsor. An off-the-cuff comment in response to a chance meeting in the corridor is helpful to no one. The desire to show the client how well things are going can occasionally outweigh common sense, so beware!

"We wonder if you could take on a couple of extra clients" is clearly good news. However, the coach needs to work through the implications of this additional work with their sponsor:

- Are there any conflicts of interest (e.g. you would be coaching both a manager and their subordinate)?

- Despite your knowledge of the organization, are you really the right person for this particular piece of work?

Although the sponsor may have a high regard for the competence of the coach, this is ultimately a decision for the coach alone. They may feel their current workload is already stretching them too far, or they may feel another coach would be a better match with a prospective participant.

Boundaries

Dealing with people issues is never easy. Executive coaching may unleash powerful feelings. The Association for Coaching[9] identifies this in its Code of Ethics, referring to the need for the executive coach to recognize both personal and professional limitations:

"Professional – with respect to whether their experience is appropriate to meet the (participant's) requirements. When this is not the case, (participants) should be referred to other appropriate services, e.g. more experienced coaches, counselors, psychotherapists or other specialist services. In particular, coaches are required to be sensitive to the possibility that some clients will require more psychological support than is normally available within the coaching remit. In these cases, referral should be made to an appropriate source of care, e.g. the (participant's) GP, a counselor or psychotherapist, psychological support services and/or agencies."

A critical element for the individual coach is understanding where the boundaries are. Reputable training programmes will always include sessions on this topic. Having a Supervisor (see Chapter 6) available as an initial reference point for a dispassionate review of your approach is a significant resource.

---

9   The Association for Coaching, Code of Ethics and Good Practice

Relationship management

The coaching process can surface a powerful mix of sensitivities around confidentiality, performance and personal concerns and fears. Perspectives and expectations may be significantly different between client and sponsor as the table below illustrates:

Sponsor perspective on executive coaching	Participant expectations of the process
Open	Confidential
Event	Process
Straightforward	Uncertain/hopeful/ challenging

Thus, what may appear as a run of the mill event for the sponsor may very well be a significant event in the life of the participant.

Effective communication throughout the process, as outlined at the initial three-way meeting, can significantly diminish these differences. The problems start when something is promised and does not materialize – for example, in an organization with a number of individuals being coached, there was an agreement for a monthly update on meetings held and an overview of topics discussed. When staff changes meant this got forgotten for a couple of months, what was an essentially administrative challenge, became elevated to a policy issue in the eyes of the sponsor. Clearly the coach needs to remember who the stakeholders in the process are and engage them. This does not mean sacrificing confidentiality – it is good practice. Over time it is also likely to lead to a satisfied sponsor who will recommend you to others!

Spotting danger signals

Direct or indirect comments from the sponsor about 'What is going on' should set the alarm bells going. Less obvious may be difficulty in finding time in the sponsor's diary to review progress.

The challenge for the coach is to continually reflect on how the process is working and to offer the client the opportunity to review the relationship.

Managing risks

The following checklist – whilst basic – is an easy way to mitigate many of these risks. It is imperative that documentation is kept up to date, and kept under lock and key. This includes:

- Copies of the proposal and work plan.
- Copies of interview notes.
- Copies of correspondence and telephone conversations.
- Copies of all client reports.
- An accurate record of all time spent.
- Copies of receipts and bills.
- Working notes.
- A formal record of signing off the coaching.

Without this information any difference of opinion over what was delivered, as opposed to that which was expected, may become acrimonious. Equally, if the coach is a subcontractor, they will need to justify time spent to their employer.

It is also good practice to check your work diary on a frequent basis and reconfirm appointments at least a day in advance!

Insufficient resources/support

When a participant contacts their coach they expect a prompt response. After all, that's why they engaged this particular coach! A coach operating as a sole practitioner should be able to mitigate this risk by ensuring that their participants know of scheduled holidays and other events. A firm which has grown quickly from a one person outfit or one which makes use of a number of associates, may be at greater risk. For example, have office procedures and administration kept pace with growth? How are associates commitments coordinated?

There is another angle on this. How do associates see their relationship with their 'employer'? Whilst they may have very good relationships with their sponsors and associates, how well do they feel they are treated by their coaching firm? Poor coordination of their diaries will not only cost them potential fees, but may also damage their reputation.

Work being overlooked

This is the most visible – and memorable – consequence of poor management. It would be surprising if anyone reading this book had not, at sometime in their career, missed a deadline or arrived late at a meeting. If this book serves no other purpose the previous sentence may have just reminded you of something you must complete by the end of today!

Issues for the internal coach

The role of internal coach is becoming more prevalent inside organizations. There are a number of reasons for this:

- A realization that coaching does actually deliver benefits has prompted internal discussions as to whether "we do this ourselves"

- An unfortunate subset of the first point is the additional – and mistaken – belief that "we'll save money too"

- The emergence of coaching firms providing training for internal coaches has created an opportunity

- An awareness that coaching skills are very useful generic additions to any managers' portfolio

That said, there are clearly some issues that both the individual and the organization need to resolve:

- What exactly does an internal coach do?

- What skills are required in addition to the core coaching skills?

- What type of person is likely to be successful?

- What are the boundaries within which they will operate?

It may well be that the initial conversation is prompted by an individual who would like to get involved as an internal coach rather than a sudden burst of corporate enthusiasm for a coaching culture.

As an individual how do you go about building a presence and differentiating yourself from external coaches? Any form of internal consulting role will experience the following pressures:

- Time – how will success in acquiring new clients impact on your current role.

- And the converse – if you fail to win any internal clients where does that leave you?

- Role conflict in terms of combining a line role with that of an executive coach.

- Some managers may have concerns about the confidentiality of an insider working with their team members.

- Is this a long-term move with a future internally or will it be seen as a signal that you would really like to leave the organization.

Additionally, as an insider you cannot walk away from your sponsor. Whilst large consulting firms will often espouse the notion that 'good consultants say no to bad business', this is a considerable personal challenge to a lone internal coach.

For those readers contemplating this move the following checklist is worth working through in some detail.

Issue	Implications?
How much and on what does your organization currently spend on people consultancy?	This can be a surprisingly difficult number to tease out! It will provide a sense of the internal market
How much of this work is in the area of personal development consulting?	i.e. one to one
What is the organizations experience of coaching?	This includes the use and impact of coaching
What level of satisfaction is there with the services provided?	High may mean awareness is high too; but also means stiff competition!
What type/number of coaches are currently used?	Is there any form of beauty parade?
Why are they used?	Experts/ know the business/previously worked with the CEO?
What opportunities are there for internal coaching?	Opportunity does not equal certainty!
Who would be a great sponsor?	What will it take to get them to give you a chance?

Testing the market

It would be surprising if the answers to the grid above provided an absolutely compelling case for working as an internal coach. Even if the economic arguments are robust, what are the unspoken barriers that need to be overcome? A useful way of addressing these issues is through the use of surveys. They can provide both a reason to make contact with the potential customer base, and provide data and opinions that are invaluable in formulating a business proposition.

Here is an example of a questionnaire developed by one potential internal coach:

Dear colleagues

I am currently conducting some research on the extent to which executive coaching is used, or likely to be used within our organization. As you may be aware, many other organizations have found coaching has helped their managers:

- by giving them a greater ability to give and receive constructive performance feedback;

- identify areas where subordinates' performance could be helped by one to one coaching;

- by providing an insight into how learning takes place in the organization;

- by providing the tools to improve team performance; and

- enhancing their skills as facilitators.

To this end I would be grateful if you would take the time to complete the survey attached. It should take no more than 15 minutes and your responses will be used to develop recommendations for discussion by the executive team.

I would be more than happy to meet with you if you need any further information before completing the survey or please give me a call on... All responses will be treated as confidential and all respondents will receive a summary of the results.

For the purpose of the survey executive coaching is: 'The non-directive process by which the coach helps the coachee fulfill their potential.'

Have you ever purchased or received executive coaching?

If yes, please provide a brief description:

- Purpose/objectives
- How many hours were spent on the coaching?
- Were the objectives achieved?
- If not, why?
- What was the cost of the coaching (per hour or per day?)
- Are you currently using an executive coach or expecting to use one within the next year?
- Outside your own area, in what other departments/circumstances do you believe executive coaching could be useful here?
- If no, do you see any areas where you believe coaching could be useful here?
- What would you anticipate the benefits to be?

Continued over...

How will you market yourself?

Having tested the market, what can you do to exploit the potential opportunities you have identified? In theory these opportunities should be available to an external provider. However, at this point only you may realize they exist! Additionally, the person on the spot will generally have greater access to key people – or know someone who does. It is also much easier to set up meetings with potential purchasers and clients when you are part of the same organization. You may know their PA and have worked with or for them. As external coaches will know, potential sales meetings with organizations frequently get postponed at the last minute as business priorities shift.

An internal survey not only gives the internal coach a perspective on the internal market, it also provides the material for:

- One-to-one meetings to debrief the results to key stakeholders

- A workshop for senior managers to review the findings

It would be naïve not to involve the HR team in both the preparation and follow-up to any survey, since:

- they could be an important ally;

- they can give you an insight into what has been attempted, or rejected in the past; and

- it will provide you with an opportunity to test out your thinking.

The role of HR in the internal coaching environment

Some CEOs and HR Directors argue that the role of the internal coach is part and parcel of their everyday role. These advocates appear to be in a minority, although paradoxically probably not a minority of those who are believers in the usefulness of the executive coaching process. In reality, whatever the disposition of the CEO and enthusiasm of the function, there will be limits to the opportunities available to HR. These are set by potential participants rather than HR and will be the consequence of a number of factors:

- The overall standing of HR within the organization and level of confidence in their ability

- The personal credibility of the individual who would be the coach and level of confidence in their integrity

- The issue/context within which executive coaching may be required

From the HR perspective there are issues of both commitment and capability. The dilemma facing the HR function was once described as the difference between a surgeon and a physician: "the learning and development team is the physician – they believe in non-invasive treatment and think talking will resolve everything; the operational and shared service side is the surgeon – if there's a problem (person) remove it". In reality HR needs to be seen as the business partner with the expertise to identify people problems and opportunities, and deal with them. Is this compatible with performing the role of executive coach? The answer is both yes and no!

It is clear that what may be seen by 'customers' as executive coaching is in reality facilitation. For example, is the HR Director asked to comment on the modus operandi of Board meetings fulfilling the requirements of executive coach or facilitator? Almost always the latter, the more so if the individual is a Board member, and if not they are still an insider.

In working with high potential individuals on their career development are they truly impartial? This is not a criticism but an acknowledgement that 'going with the flow' of a coaching conversation is exceptionally difficult if a participant expresses the hope that they will be able to work in Brazil, when only the day before they were seen as the ideal candidate for a role in India.

On the positive side, the HR function – or to be more accurate – those within it who have the appropriate skills, experience and commitment are confronted every day with opportunities to coach the organization through the consequences of globalization, acquisition, downsizing, restructuring and many, many more changes. In reality, the hat they wear in this context is more that of strategic change agent than executive coach.

SIX
What to look for in a coach

By way of getting the bad news out of the way in one swoop, this chapter begins with a look at those types of executive coach who are better avoided! Having disposed of them we then look at some criteria for the sponsor and participant to consider when seeking an executive coach.

Coaches to avoid

The motto 'buyers beware' applies to any purchase. One of the aims of this book is to ensure that buyers of executive coaching are more aware of their needs and how coaching may help. The types of coach identified below are very rare, but they do sometimes emerge from the shadows:

The trophy coach

"We think you've reached a point in your career where a coach would be of great help. As you probably know a number of very senior managers here have coaches." Is this potential recipient being rewarded or punished? Certainly having your own coach is the modern day of having the keys to the executive cloakroom in some corporate circles. It may be apocryphal but the story of the City traders, who were lamenting the need to accept a coach or they would not be considered for promotion, will resonate with many.

The terminator coach

The ethical issues of using coaching to 'help' someone decide on their future were discussed above. Beware, therefore, of the terminator coach where an individual is offered a coach as part of outplacement by stealth.

The coach as surrogate manager

This is a variant on the 'terminator', where the boss tells you: "As you know I'll be away on secondment for the next six months. Don't worry, a chap from a coaching outfit has been hired to give you some help if you need it."

The adhesive coach

This individual tends to emphasize how expert **they** are. They alone are able to help you: "Never mind the chemistry, just trust me."

The coach on the couch

The coach on the couch offers huge amounts of empathy but little positive help. Probably confusing intuition with judgment they will relive their experience through yours: "That's just what happened to me – here's what I did…"

The absentee coach

The absentee coach prefers to coach via the telephone rather than face-to-face. They see themselves as so phenomenally successful, you should consider yourself lucky to get even this.

The borderless coach

With little sense of boundaries or ethics this type of coach blithely goes where others will not. Lacking technical training and experience, they are best avoided.

What works?

So, what **should** we look for? These are the criteria that sponsors regularly apply:

- Deemed to be capable of operating at the most senior levels in the organization, and with a track-record to prove it.

- Flexibility in approach – i.e. not wedded to one particular 'ology' at the expense of flexibility when required.

- Focused on ensuring every programme achieves closure.

- Demonstrates empathy with both the organizational context and the participants needs.

In identifying which coaches may meet these criteria a number of approaches are available, ranging from contacting one of the organizations listed in this book, to conducting your own research on the internet. Additional sources of information and referral are your own colleagues and professional networks. It would also be very surprising if the organization had not been targeted and sent mail shots by at least one provider of executive coaching over the last year.

This research will produce a number of coaches worth seeing. Some organizations lose an opportunity when they convince themselves that "there's no immediate need at present; we'll hold a beauty parade when there is". Looked at another way, reviewing the approach and perspective of a number of coaches will give you a chance to test out your thinking on your current needs, and at no cost!

Who to see?

Having assembled a shortlist, it is always worth inviting the selected individuals/firms to send you information on the following in advance:

Factor	Implications
Size of coaching firm	Size isn't everything but how many coaches do they use on a regular basis?
Quality of coaches	How are coaches chosen; what are the minimum training requirements; where were the coach(es) trained; what continuous personal development is offered?
Experience	Ask for detailed CVs of each coach
Track-record	Is this their first time in your sector/function?
What arrangements are in place for supervision?	Do they have access to a professional with whom to review their performance?
What is the 'house' approach	This may be NLP focused; based on the GROW model
Qualifications	Occupational psychologist/psychotherapist/counselor/executive coach/other?
Fee structure	How flexible is the structure; is it based on coaching completed or coaching committed to by the organization; what is the hourly rate?
Availability/logistics	You are in London, they are based 300 miles away – will this work?

Factor	Implications
Professional development	How do they keep in touch with the executive coaching community/membership of professional associations?
Quality control	How is this managed? Ask for a description of the process used.

The Federal Consulting Group has developed a very helpful 'Guide to Executive Coaching'[10] which discusses some of the considerations executives will need to think about when choosing a coach:

- "The coach's typical clients and developmental issues – Has the coach worked with situations similar to mine?

- General technique or approach to coaching – Am I willing to work within these techniques or approaches? Do I prefer to work face-to-face, by phone, or e-mail? How flexible am I on the 'meeting' format?

- Experience coaching Federal managers – Has the coach worked with Federal managers so that he/she is familiar with the dynamics unique to Federal organizations or by my organization in particular?

- Business/organizational knowledge – does the coach understand the business/organizational issues related to my situation?

- Values – sensitivity to confidentiality, ethics, and freedom from gender and culture bias – am I comfortable that the coach can work for my best interest?

---

10 The FCG Executive Coaching Guide – Steps for a Successful Coaching Partnership – March 2002

- Interpersonal skills – listening, straightforwardness, rapport, trust, warmth, compassion, humor – is the coach someone I can trust? Does the coach listen to understand?

- Assessment skills and awareness of instruments applicable to your situation – what other information will the coach use to assist me?

- Flexibility and the ability to work effectively with a broad range of executives – my issues involve relationships with other executives; can the coach work with me effectively and help me understand how to work effectively with them?

- Ability to plan, conceptualize, implement and manage a coaching relationship over time – how will the coach keep me accountable for results and assure that I keep making progress?

- Demonstrated knowledge of learning theories and the dynamics of change – does the coach understand the personality and temperament issues related to my situation or organization?

- Credibility and authenticity – can I trust this coach to be honest with me?

- Political savvy – is the coach savvy enough to understand the politics of my situation?

Not all of the above will be revealed through words during an interview with the coach. Some are part of the 'chemistry' that we may or may not feel when we meet the coach and it may take at least one coaching session to decide."

Is who you see, who you get?

The fragmented nature of the executive coaching market has been referred to earlier. The coach you see will probably fall into one of the following categories:

Sole practitioner

Here, it could be somewhat churlishly argued, what you see is all that you get! The reasons for the preponderance of sole practitioners in the coaching marketplace can be attributed to the following:

- Very experienced senior executives who have decided to distance themselves from the internal politics of organizations, and instead focus all their energies on client needs by working for themselves.

- Individuals who, for whatever reason, have determined how much they need to earn in a year and who consequently restrict the number of coaching assignments they are prepared to undertake accordingly.

Cooperatives

Some sole practitioners have formed loose alliances with other coaches to:

- Enable them to get involved in larger coaching assignments.

- Enable the participant to have a greater choice.

- Provide a professional forum within which to review standards, quality and the progress of assignments.

Freelance subcontractor

There are a significant number of freelance coaches who are subcontracted to other, larger brands. In part this is a legitimate response to the unpredictability of a market which can move from feast to famine, and to control overhead costs and hence keep fee increases in check. Generally these coaches will have signed a non-compete agreement with their 'host' firm and will have been required to demonstrate that they possess the skills, experience and qualifications required to represent the firm.

Partner, salaried employee

These people may have once been sole practitioners or freelancers, and decided to move into a corporate structure. Larger firms should be able to offer more choice in terms of the number of coaches and the range of experience they possess. However, remember that a firm with coaching as its core business is going to be 'large' in the UK market if it has more than half a dozen full-time staff.

Consultancies

Last, but by no means least are the many consultancies which offer coaching alongside other deliverables, ranging from HR consulting to search to change management. These may have tens, hundreds or thousands of consultants. In many cases, executive coaching will not feature as part of their repertoire. Where it does, check out whether what's on offer is facilitation – since some consultants clearly think this is executive coaching!

Quality control

Apart from the issue of whether who you see is who you get, will you get what you want? Most of us would hope that a robust process, agreed arrangements for communicating with the sponsor, and a written proposal with terms of reference, would ensure high quality executive coaching. However in a setting where more than one coach is at work, a coaching firm will often assign another coach as the person responsible for managing the relationship. This would typically include meeting with the sponsor every three months and liaising on a regular basis with the executive coaches delivering the work.

Whether operating as part of a team, or working as a sole practitioner, a very useful tool for both coach and participant is illustrated below. After each coaching session the participant is invited to complete the form, reflect upon it, and use it in preparing for the next session. The coach does likewise. For each, it represents both a tracker of intent and actual progress, as well as a means for the participant to surface any concerns over the process and their coach.

TRACKING THE PROCESS	DATE	SESSION /

WHAT ARE YOUR GOALS FOR THE COACHING PROGRAMME?

WHAT WILL SUCCESS LOOK LIKE?

WHAT ARE THE INSIGHTS YOU GAINED FROM TODAY'S COACHING SESSION?

WHAT BROUGHT THESE ABOUT?

WHAT WILL YOU BE DOING AS A RESULT?

HOW DO YOU FEEL WE ARE BOTH WORKING TOGETHER?

> **WHAT WOULD MAKE THE PROCESS MORE EFFECTIVE FOR YOU?**

> **WHAT DO YOU NEED TO DO TO GET THIS TO HAPPEN?**

> **WHAT DOES YOUR COACH NEED TO DO?**

The tracker tool can be used as a preface to each coaching session, or provide the basis for a short catch-up between coach and participant between sessions. It also gives the participant another signal that they own the process.

Supervision

The question of supervision for executive coaches is important for both the professional development of the coach and the appropriate management of the coaching process. It assists the management of boundaries and provides a means for an executive coach to test out their perspective on the effectiveness of their approach:

> *"By its very nature, coaching makes considerable demands upon coaches who may become over-involved, ignore some important point or have undermining doubts about their own abilities. It is difficult, if not sometimes impossible, to be objective about one's coaching and the opportunity to discuss the coaching work in confidence with a suitable person is invaluable."*

The less experience the coach has, the more experience the supervisor needs. Supervisors should be sufficiently experienced and qualified in coaching or in a closely related field for others to have confidence in their professional skills.[11]

Commitment to Continuing Professional Development

How does your coach keep in good professional shape? A supervisor may have a part to play, as will membership of professional associations. A good example from the USA is that developed by the Federal Consulting Group, which is a franchise of the US Department of the Treasury. It has established 'The Coaches Community of Learning' which is a network for senior executive coaches who serve clients in the federal government.

"The group shares best practices, collaborates on goals and discusses recent coaching work. It assesses the impact of coaching on clients and their organizations. The COL extends its knowledge through presentations by coaches, thought-leaders on seminal work on the frontiers of coaching. The COL is held quarterly and is free."

On a personal basis it is important for the coach to reflect upon and review every session. A self-review tracker for the coach's personal use provides the framework for doing this:

PERSONAL COACHING TRACKER

DATE	PARTICIPANT	SESSION /

DID I ENSURE PARTICIPANT OWNERSHIP OF PROCESS?

---

11 Association for Coaching: Coaching Supervision Information Sheet

DID I USE APPROPRIATE QUESTIONS?

HOW MUCH DID I LISTEN?

- For interest?
- For understanding?

HOW WELL DID I FOLLOW THE PARTICIPANT'S INTEREST?

DID I ENSURE WE HAD AN AGREED GOAL FOR THE SESSION? AND AGREED ACTIONS BEFORE THE NEXT SESSION?

SEVEN

What to look for as a potential coach

This chapter reviews the key issues anyone contemplating a move into executive coaching should consider.

- What are the reasons for your interest in executive coaching?
- How much do you know about executive coaching?
- Market research
- Training
- Working as an executive coach

What are the reasons for your interest in executive coaching?

There are countless answers to this question. They include:

- Experienced management consultants looking to widen their repertoire
- Recently downsized senior managers reviewing their next move
- Human Resources managers who would like to work for themselves
- Line managers wishing to add coaching skills to their toolbox
- "I want to make a lot of money"

For each and every person there will be a different set of criteria against which they need to make choices about their future. In reality someone seeing executive coaching solely as a money making proposition is likely to be disappointed. So are their clients!

How much do you know about executive coaching?

You may have first-hand experience, having commissioned executive coaching or perhaps been a recipient of coaching yourself. You may have colleagues who have been either a sponsor or participant. Or your first contact with executive coaching may have been through this book.

Whatever your background, please do not make any irrevocable decisions without further research! Executive Coaching is not a field in which everyone can excel; it requires more than enthusiasm to be successful. There are two principal routes available to help you test out your suitability: undertaking a training course and doing some practical market research. These are examined below. However, a bigger issue for many people contemplating a career move is taking a rational look at whether they will be able to make a success of working for themselves. In this context executive coaching may be one of many opportunities under consideration. In these circumstances, advice on all aspects of starting and then maintaining you own business may be an important precursor to the actions outlined below.

Training to be an executive coach

A better heading might be 'Using training as a means of discovering whether you are – or can become – competent to be an executive coach and whether you are likely to enjoy it.' As a potential coach commented after a training programme, "It's been really useful to me personally and I'm definitely a better listener now. I also realize that, whilst I believe I am a competent executive coach, it doesn't give me the buzz I expected".

There are now a wide range of programmes, courses and workshops which claim to provide training in the skills of executive coaching. In reviewing what's available the following are important differentiators:

- What are the entry criteria?
- How is the programme structured?
- How much supervised practice does the programme include?
- Does successful completion lead to a recognized qualification?
- How many people will be on each programme?
- What is the ratio of trainers to students?
- Alumni and faculty
- Value for money

What are the entry criteria?

This point is raised not to turn executive coaching into some form of elitist profession, but as a safeguard to the potential trainee. Although Groucho Marks remarked that, "Who'd want to be a member of any club that would have me", any provider of training has a duty of care to their trainees. So be wary if there is no selection process for a training course. Without this it is impossible to assess the potential and commitment an individual possesses.

How is the programme structured?

Is the programme a mix of theory and practice? How flexible is the structure? Some courses are based on a modular format which includes an introductory module, which could provide an opportunity to put a toe in the coaching water without any risk of longer-term commitment and outlay.

How much supervised practice is included?

Without observed practice, feedback and more practice it is impossible to acquire the skills an executive coach requires. At least half the time needs to be allocated to this key activity.

Does successful completion lead to recognized qualification?

Organizations awarding their own qualifications only have to satisfy themselves. Links with educational establishments add both scrutiny and credibility to a qualification. They will also ensure that completion includes assessment of theory and practical application, rather than a meaningless attendance certificate.

How many people will be on each programme?

A balance needs to be struck.

Is the programme focused on the effective development of between eight to twenty participants or much larger numbers?

What is the ratio of trainers to students?

Fifty students and only one lecturer sends any prospective participant a clear message about how much supervised practice there will be!

Alumni and faculty

Find out more about the backgrounds of previous students and what they are doing now. Are those providing your training also currently working as executive coaches? It certainly helps if most are, but specialist inputs from occupational psychologists for whom coaching may be a minor part of their business are also valuable. Equally, do clients get invited to give their experience and expectations?

Value for money

Inevitably, value for money depends on what you want from the programme and whether that's what you get. What other resources such as library access or 'master classes' are included in the price? Are there other, additional costs for residential parts of the programme? If you are aiming to become an internal coach will your employer pay some or all of the costs?

Market research

For someone wanting to test out whether executive coaching is right for them, talking to people already in the business is a great way to get a feel for what's on offer and how it's delivered.

The organizations listed in the **Further Information** section are a good place to start. A web search will generate many more potential sources of information. Ideally, try to meet with a cross section of coaches from sole practitioner to senior people in larger firms. A short letter asking for a brief discussion to review prospects within the coaching profession should do the trick.

Working as an executive coach

It may be that opportunities to get your first experience of delivering executive coaching come along as a consequence of contacts made on your training course. Others may not be so lucky, so they will need to approach other coaches and firms for work, or market themselves directly. Many individuals who have gone solo have done so on the basis of work generated through their existing network of contacts, who have then recommended them to other organizations.

As noted earlier, issues other than enthusiasm need to be considered here. For example, you will need professional advice on the appropriate legal and tax structure for your business.

When looking at working for another outfit keep in your mind that you need to be able to answer two key questions: "What will they get from me; and what will I gain from them?"

Think through what 'gain' really means to you at this stage in your life and career:

- Are you looking for experience that will prepare you to strike out on your own in the future?
- Are you looking for a secure job in a stable organization?

Below is a list of things to check out; it can be hard to break into the executive coaching market, so don't let concern over upsetting a potential employer lead you to neglect your own due diligence!

History and structure

How old is the business? What is the ownership structure?

Talk to the executive coaches already working there

By there very nature executive coaching firms and executive coaches are somewhat 'virtual'. An empty office may indicate that everyone is very busy – marketing, training and conducting coaching sessions. But persevere and try to fix up a few meetings over a coffee. These are the people you will be working with, and upon whom you may well depend for referrals so find out what makes them tick!

Ask how often the team get together to discuss marketing opportunities and to review the progress of coaching engagements. The aim is for you to get a sense of how this firm manages itself, so it's also important to…

…Meet the back office staff

How is billing and administration handled? How client focused is the atmosphere? How tidy is the office? How is the database kept up to date? Who coordinates diaries?

Remuneration

How will you pay be structured? Will there be any form of bonus? When will you get paid – on a regular retainer basis or only after the firm has been paid? What arrangements exist for covering your expenses? And what information do you need to provide to ensure that you are paid?

Volume of work

Many market facing organizations tend to be somewhat over-expansive in describing work about to be won. Satisfy yourself on how many hours work you can expect in your first three months.

Type of work

What type of coaching will you actually be doing and what level of commitment will be required from you? Will you be the lead coach or used on an intermittent basis to assist other coaches. Will you be expected to turn up, do the coaching and provide regular progress reports to the office or play a more active role, such as spotting opportunities to sell new work? There is no right or wrong answer here but you do need to identify what approach and pattern of work suits you.

Unexpected costs

You will almost certainly be responsible for your own Professional Indemnity insurance. What else might there be?

Continuing Professional Development

The more you are involved in developing others, the less likely you, or your employer, are to invest in your own development! How will this firm assist your professional development? Some firms make a point of running regular events on topical themes or to review each others case load.

Existing clients

Ask if it's possible to meet a couple of existing clients. A good coaching firm will have good relationships with its clients so this may be easier than you might at first think.

Induction

Ask how you will be introduced to your colleagues and sponsors/clients. If no one has any idea or is vague, does this mean you will be left to fend for yourself?

EIGHT
Making this book work for you

This chapter identifies issues of relevance to anyone contemplating the use of executive coaching for their organization or themselves. It provides a framework for individuals to use in reviewing whether coaching might be of use to them personally, and provides further information on some of the organizations providing training for coaches.

Does your organization need executive coaching?

Or to be more accurate, are there senior individuals in the organization who might benefit from individual or team coaching?

We have reviewed a variety of situations in which executive coaching may be an appropriate intervention, including:

- Project teams.
- Integration teams.
- Executive teams.
- Newly promoted senior managers/new hires.
- Senior international assignees.

Whilst the underlying purpose of executive coaching is the fulfillment of potential, this may go hand in hand with the mitigation of risk. For example, enhancing the performance of a project team will ensure delivery for the organization and develop the individual members of the team. Equally, executive coaching for a newly arrived international assignee will speed up their assimilation of the requirements of their new role and significantly reduce the risk of an early – and costly – return home.

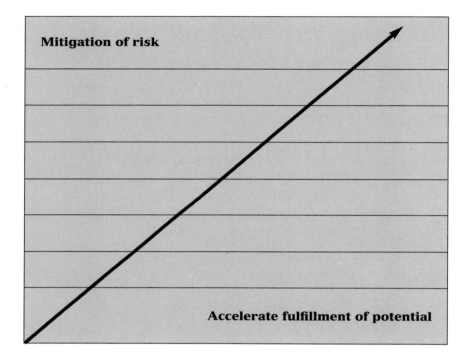

Using the grid above may pinpoint particularly significant areas where coaching may help your own organization at the present time. To support this indicator there will be many other sources of information available including:

- Training needs analyses.
- Performance reviews.
- 360 degree feedback.
- Opinion surveys.
- Exit interviews.
- Labor turnover analyses.

- Succession planning.
- The business plan.

There may be recurring themes which emerge from these tools and processes such as concerns over where the future leadership of the organization will come from; or an over-reliance on the same – small – cadre of individuals to run every high priority project.

Organizational impact

Any assessment of impact needs to be based on the organizational imperatives and individual goals that prompted the coaching to be commissioned in the first place. For example:

- To improve the working of the international assignee scheme by accelerating the assimilation of assignees into their host environment.
- To enable x to review their approach to managing their unit and identify and adopt learning strategies to improve their effectiveness.

Some organizations have their own processes for assessing whether their investment in executive coaching has delivered an appropriate return. However, one survey found that only 19% of organizations formally evaluate the impact of coaching.[12]

The approaches that can be utilized range from informal conversations to structured interviews, to anonymous feedback via questionnaires. Ideally, it is helpful to have the approach agreed in advance of any coaching. One person responsible for monitoring executive coaching within an organization noted:

"I joined just as the programme started. I was not involved in the initial selection of coaches and consequently developed a set of measures and questions for assessing impact 'after the event'. This caused some

---

12 "The Future of Executive Coaching" Hay Group 2002

problems: in part because each of the coaches claimed to have their own approach and also because some of the participants were a bit coy about discussing what they wanted to get out of the process with me. Had we had a framework in position at the start the coaches would have been able to bear it in mind and known what would be required. Equally, the participants would have been aware of our expectations and the impor- tance to the organization of being able to conduct a thorough review. There was nothing in the framework that compromised confidentiality, but there was definitely some suspicion on the part of one or two colleagues."

To return to a theme recurring through this book, it is self-evident that if the organization doesn't know what coaching is happening, it is difficult to assess the impact! As a minimum therefore, the following information would seem vital as the prerequisite for tracking purpose, outcomes and impact:

Overall

- Participant
- Current role
- Sponsor (and line manager if different)
- Type of coaching programme
- Number of sessions or time purchased
- Purpose of coaching and anticipated outcomes and criteria for identifying success
- Anticipated completion date

> **For each session**
>
> - Session 1 of ...
> - Purpose of session
> - Tools/processes used
> - Outcomes
> - Actions agreed

Personal commitment

Finally, are you ready to personally benefit from executive coaching? The FCG[13] suggests the following commitments are important if the participant is to maximize the benefit of the coaching experience:

- Assume ownership of your learning. Use your coach to help you maximize your learning style
- Be forthright about what is and isn't working in coaching sessions
- Engage wholeheartedly in the agreed upon coaching assignments
- Take required actions for learning and reflect on those actions
- Maintain an open attitude toward experimenting with new perspectives and behaviors
- Willingly be vulnerable and take risks
- Focus on your growth within your current and future organizational role
- Transfer learning gained through coaching to your day to day work

---

13 Federal Consulting Group: "The FCG Executive Coaching Guide" March 2002

- Exchange feedback with your coach about the helpfulness of the feedback
- Seek feedback from others in the organization about the results of your coaching"

Finally

If this book has a mantra it is that executive coaching is a powerful process if used for the right reasons in an appropriate context by a qualified practitioner.

It is simply not possible for someone to make themselves an effective executive coach without professional training and supervised practice no matter how strong their commitment. The book aspires to be the starting point for would-be coaches and participants and sponsors to know what to look for and what to ask!

Further information

The European Mentoring and Coaching Council
Sherwood House
7 Oxhey Road
Watford WD19 4QF
+44(0)7000 234682
www.emccouncil.com

The EMCC is a not for profit organization which exists to promote good practice and the expectation of good practice in mentoring and coaching across Europe.

Appendix 1 contains the EMCC "Vision and Aims."

International Coach Federation
1444 'I' Street NW Suite 700
Washington
DC 20005
888 423 3131
www.thecoachfederation.org

ICF is the largest non-profit professional association worldwide of personal and business coaches with more than 6000 members in over 145 chapters in 30 countries.

The Chartered Institute of Personnel and Development
CIPD House
Camp Road
London SW19 4UX
+44(0)208 2633434
www.cipd.co.uk

The CIPD offers an Advanced Certificate in Coaching and Mentoring in association with the Oxford School of Coaching and Mentoring.

The School of Coaching
Peter Runge House
3 Carlton House Terrace
London
SW1 5DG
+44(0)207 004 7149
www.theschoolofcoaching.com

The School offers a Certificate of Professional Development in Executive Coaching, accredited by The University of Strathclyde Center for Lifelong Learning.

The Association for Coaching
66 Church Road
London W7 1LB
www.associationforcoaching.com

The Association is an independent non-profit organization with the goal to promote best practice, raise awareness and standards across the UK coaching industry whilst providing value added benefits to its members – whether they are Coaches or Organizations involved in coaching.

The Association has an online Directory of Coaches available to non-members.

The British Psychological Society

The BPS launched the Psychological Testing Centre in 2002 to provide information about tests and testing.

Psychological Testing Centre

St Andrews House
48 Princess Road East
Leicester LE1 7DR
0116 2529530
www.psychtesting.org.uk

The British Association for Counselling and Psychotherapy

BACP House
35-37 Albert Street
Rugby, Warwickshire
CV21 2SG
0870 4435252
www.bacp.co.uk

The vision of the BACP is to "lead the effort to make counselling and psychotherapy widely recognized as a profession whose purpose is widely understood by the general public."

Project management

Avanza Partnership
www.avanzapartnership.com

Psychometrics

Jim Barrett
Chartered Psychologists and Test Publishers
37 Dorset Road
Merton Park
London SW19 3EZ
0208 544 0251
www.psychometrictests.com

APPENDIX ONE
British Association for Counselling and Psychotherapy

Personal qualities

The BACP sees the 'personal qualities' to which counsellors and psychotherapists should aspire as being:

- **Empathy**: the ability to communicate understanding of another person's experience from that person's perspective.

- **Sincerity**: a personal commitment to consistency between what is professed and what is done.

- **Integrity**: commitment to being moral in dealings with others, personal straightforwardness, honesty and coherence.

- **Resilience**: the capacity to work with the client's concerns without being personally diminished.

- **Respect**: showing appropriate esteem to others and their under-standing of themselves.

- **Humility**: the ability to assess accurately and acknowledge one's own strengths and weaknesses.

- **Competence**: the effective deployment of the skills and knowledge needed to do what is required.

- **Fairness**: the consistent application of appropriate criteria to inform decisions and actions.

- **Wisdom**: possession of sound judgment that informs practice.

- **Courage**: the capacity to act in spite of known fears, risks and uncertainty.

APPENDIX TWO

The British Psychological Society Code of Good Practice for Psychological Testing

People who use psychological tests for assessment are expected by the BPS to:

Responsibility for Competence

1. Take steps to ensure that they are able to meet all the standards of competence defined by the Society for the relevant Certificate(s) of Competence in Psychological Testing, and to endeavor, where possible, to develop and enhance their competence as test users.

2. Monitor the limits of their competence in psychometric testing and not to offer services which lie outside their competence nor encourage or cause others to do so.

Procedures and Techniques

3. only use tests in conjunction with other assessment methods and only when their use can be supported by the available technical information

4. administer, score and interpret tests in accordance with the instructions provided by the test distributor and to the standards defined by the Society

5. store test materials securely and to ensure that no unqualified person has access to them

6. keep test results securely, in a form suitable for developing norms, validation, and monitoring for bias

Client Welfare

7. obtain the informed consent of potential test takers, or, where appropriate their legitimate representatives, making sure that they understand why the tests will be used, what will be done with their results and who will be provided with access to them

8. ensure that all test takers are well informed and well prepared for the test session, and that all have had access to practice or familiarization materials where appropriate

9. give due consideration to factors such as gender, ethnicity, age, disability and special needs, educational background and level of ability in using and interpreting the results of tests

10. provide the test taker or other authorized persons with feedback about the results in a form which makes clear the implications of the results, is clear and in a style appropriate to their level of understanding

11. ensure that confidentiality is respected and that test results are stored securely, are not accessible to unauthorized or unqualified persons and are not used for any purposes other than those agreed with the test user.

APPENDIX THREE
The European Mentoring and Coaching Council

Vision and aims

EMCC exists to promote good practice and the expectation of good practice in mentoring and coaching across Europe.

It aims to achieve this through:

- The on-going development and application of a widely agreed statement of ethical and professional standards in coaching and mentoring.

- Creation and support of forums, using traditional and new media, for dialogue and mutual learning across the spectrum of mentoring and coaching.

- Lobbying, where appropriate, to support socially responsible coaching and mentoring in all sectors of employment and community development.

- Stimulation of research and benchmarking.

- Maintenance of an extensive library of materials on coaching and mentoring.

- Respecting the wide range of perspectives and approaches to mentoring, coaching and the complementary professions that may be appropriate for different contexts.

- Recognizing the continuous professional development needs, and valid options for meeting these needs, of all levels of experience of coaching and mentoring, from full-time professionals to occasional volunteers, within an appropriate framework of standards.

- Recognizing the needs of consumers of coaching and mentoring services for an authoritative, impartial and objective source of information on the quality of service provision available in their geographical area.

- Improving communications between providers of mentoring and coaching services:
  - Their clients and customers, both individual and organizational.
  - The academics engaged in the search for good practice in coaching and mentoring.

- Providing a membership forum for all those involved in the wide variety of the applications of coaching and mentoring, while placing its greatest emphasis on those areas, which are not already well represented by other bodies.

- Ensure that our working practices and professional relationships reflect the underlying values expressed in this statement and are kept under regular review.

Bibliography

These are the books I have found it helpful to dip into for insight and inspiration:

- 'Effective Coaching', Miles Downey, Texere
- 'The Book of Me', Barrie Pearson and Neil Thomas, Thorogood
- 'The Fifth Discipline Fieldbook', Peter Senge et al, Nicholas Brearly Publishing
- 'The NLP Coach', Ian McDermott and Wendy Jago, Piatkus
- 'The Boundaryless Organization', Ron Ashkenas et al, Jossey-Bass
- 'High Flyers', Morgan W McCall, HBS Press
- 'Making Sense of Emotional Intelligence', M. Higgs, and V Dulewicz
- 'Creating the Resilient Organization', Edward Deevey, Prentice Hall
- 'What Really Works', William Joyce, Nitin Nohria, Bruce Roberson, Harper Business
- 'Coaching Across Cultures', Philippe Rosinski, Nicholas Brearly Publishing
- 'Total Leadership', Jim Barrett, Kogan Page

Other titles from Thorogood

THE COMPANY DIRECTOR'S DESKTOP GUIDE

David Martin

£16.99 paperback • Published June 2004

The role of the company director is fundamental to the success of any business, yet the tasks, responsibilities and liabilities that directors' face become more demanding with every change to the law.

Written in a clear, jargon-free style, this is a comprehensive guide to the complex legislation and procedures governing all aspects of the company director's role. The author's wide experience as a Director and Secretary of a plc and consultant and author provides a manual that is expert, practical and easy to access.

THE COMPANY SECRETARY'S DESKTOP GUIDE

Roger Mason

£16.99 paperback • Published April 2004

Written in a clear, jargon-free style, this is a comprehensive guide to the complex legislation and procedures governing all aspects of the company secretary's work. The Company Secretary's role becomes more demanding with every change to the law and practice. The author's considerable experience as both Company Secretary and lecturer and author has ensured a manual that is expert, practical and easy to access.

DEVELOPING AND MANAGING TALENT

How to match talent to the role and convert it to a strength

Sultan Kermally
£12.99 paperback, £24.99 hardback
Published May 2004

Effective talent management is crucial to business development and profitability. Talent management is no soft option; on the contrary, it is critical to long-term survival.

This book offers strategies and practical guidance for finding, developing and above all keeping talented individuals. After explaining what developing talent actually means to the organization, he explores the e-dimension and the global dimension. He summarizes what the 'gurus' have to say on the development of leadership talent. Included are valuable case studies drawn from Hilton, Volkswagen, Unilever, Microsoft and others.

GURUS ON BUSINESS STRATEGY

Tony Grundy
£14.99 paperback, £24.99 hardback
Published May 2003

This book is a one-stop guide to the world's most important writers on business strategy. It expertly summarises all the key strategic concepts and describes the work and contribution of each of the leading thinkers in the field.

It goes further: it analyses the pro's and con's of many of the key theories in practice and offers two enlightening case-studies. The third section of the book provides a series of detailed checklists to aid you in the development of your own strategies for different aspects of the business.

More than just a summary of the key concepts, this book offers valuable insights into their application in practice.

SUCCESSFUL BUSINESS PLANNING

Norton Paley
£14.99 paperback, £29.99 hardback
Published June 2004

"Growth firms with a written business plan have increased their revenues 69 per cent faster over the past five years than those without a written plan."

FROM A SURVEY BY PRICEWATERHOUSECOOPERS

We know the value of planning – in theory. But either we fail to spend the time required to go through the thinking process properly, or we fail to use the plan effectively. Paley uses examples from real companies to turn theory into practice.

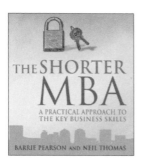

THE SHORTER MBA

A practical approach to the key business skills

Barrie Pearson and Neil Thomas
£35.00 Hardback • Published July 2004

A succinct distillation of the skills that you need to be successful in business. Most people can't afford to give up two years to study for an MBA. This pithy, practical book presents all the essential theory, practiced and techniques taught to MBA students – ideal for the busy practising executive. It is divided into three parts:

- Personal development
- Management skills
- Business development

THE A-Z OF EMPLOYMENT PRACTICE

David Martin
£19.99 paperback, £42.00 hardback
Published November 2004

This book provides comprehensive, practical guidance on personnel law and practice at a time when employers are faced with a maze of legislation, obligations and potential penalties. It provides detailed and practical advice on what to do and how to do it.

The A to Z format ensures that sections appear under individual headings for instant ease of reference. The emphasis is not so much on the law as on its implications; the advice is expert, clear and practical, with a minimum of legal references. Checklists, procedures and examples are all given as well as warnings on specific pitfalls.

MIND LAUNDRY

Gerry Kushel
£12.99 paperback. Published June 2004

A perceptive guide and set of techniques on how to get rid of messy, negative thoughts from your mind and how to ensure that it's clear and receptive to positive ones. Rid yourself of low esteem and obsessions, learn to manage your own thought processes and emotions. Understand how others see you. Present, negotiate and influence others confidently and effectively.

Thorogood also has an extensive range of reports and special briefings which are written specifically for professionals wanting expert information.

For a full listing of all Thorogood publications, or to order any title, please call Thorogood Customer Services on 020 7749 4748 or fax on 020 7729 6110. Alternatively view our website at **www.thorogood.ws**.

BUSINESS SEMINARS

Focused on developing your potential

Falconbury, the sister company to Thorogood publishing, brings together the leading experts from all areas of management and strategic development to provide you with a comprehensive portfolio of action-centred training and learning.

We understand everything managers and leaders need to be, know and do to succeed in today's commercial environment. Each product addresses a different technical or personal development need that will encourage growth and increase your potential for success.

- Practical public training programmes
- Tailored in-company training
- Coaching
- Mentoring
- Topical business seminars
- Trainer bureau/bank
- Adair Leadership Foundation

The most valuable resource in any organisation is its people; it is essential that you invest in the development of your management and leadership skills to ensure your team fulfil their potential. Investment into both personal and professional development has been proven to provide an outstanding ROI through increased productivity in both you and your team. Ultimately leading to a dramatic impact on the bottom line.

With this in mind Falconbury have developed a comprehensive portfolio of training programmes to enable managers of all levels to develop their skills in leadership, communications, finance, people management, change management and all areas vital to achieving success in today's commercial environment.

What Falconbury can offer you?

- Practical applied methodology with a proven results
- Extensive bank of experienced trainers
- Limited attendees to ensure one-to-one guidance
- Up to the minute thinking on management and leadership techniques
- Interactive training
- Balanced mix of theoretical and practical learning
- Learner-centred training
- Excellent cost/quality ratio

Falconbury In-Company Training

Falconbury are aware that a public programme may not be the solution to leadership and management issues arising in your firm. Involving only attendees from your organisation and tailoring the programme to focus on the current challenges you face individually and as a business may be more appropriate. With this in mind we have brought together our most motivated and forward thinking trainers to deliver tailored in-company programmes developed specifically around the needs within your organisation.

All our trainers have a practical commercial background and highly refined people skills. During the course of the programme they act as facilitator, trainer and mentor, adapting their style to ensure that each individual benefits equally from their knowledge to develop new skills.

Falconbury works with each organisation to develop a programme of training that fits your needs.

Mentoring and coaching

Developing and achieving your personal objectives in the workplace is becoming increasingly difficult in today's constantly changing environment. Additionally, as a manager or leader, you are responsible for guiding colleagues towards the realisation of their goals. Sometimes it is easy to lose focus on your short and long-term aims.

Falconbury's one-to-one coaching draws out individual potential by raising self-awareness and understanding, facilitating the learning and performance development that creates excellent managers and leaders. It builds renewed self-confidence and a strong sense of 'can-do' competence, contributing significant benefit to the organisation. Enabling you to focus your energy on developing your potential and that of your colleagues.

Mentoring involves formulating winning strategies, setting goals, monitoring achievements and motivating the whole team whilst achieving a much improved work life balance.

Falconbury – Business Legal Seminars

Falconbury Business Legal Seminars specialises in the provision of high quality training for legal professionals from both in-house and private practice internationally.

The focus of these events is to provide comprehensive and practical training on current international legal thinking and practice in a clear and informative format.

Event subjects include, drafting commercial agreements, employment law, competition law, intellectual property, managing an in-house legal department and international acquisitions.

For more information on all our services please contact Falconbury on +44 (0) 20 7729 6677 or visit the website at: www.falconbury.co.uk.